Forty Demons

Forty Demons

One Man's Astonishing Vision
Quest to Save the World

Mark Scott-Nash

Published by SnowDragon Publishing

E-mail: open.spaces@comcast.net

Cover and text design by Mark Scott-Nash

This isn't a camping trip, it's a shootout with the devil. I didn't come here to build campfires and look at the stars, I came out here to track something down, to kill them, one by one, forty days, forty demons...

W. B. C.

Contents

Preface

One hot afternoon in September of 2008 I was browsing a popular outdoor oriented website forum. A thread titled "My good friend went missing in Lake City..." caught my eye. As I read it I immediately recognized the desperation of the message. Decades of experience in mountain search and rescue had taught me the euphemisms used to skirt around mentioning the eight hundred pound gorilla: Suicidal individual.

I felt empathy for whomever was looking for this poor soul, but to tell you the truth, except for his implausible name, I was not intrigued. I had become jaded by seeing too many of these cases, too many suicidal parties who disappear into the mountains, only to be found dead a few days later.

That isn't what happened with Winston Branko Churchill. As the search went on over the next few weeks, there was a kind of growing energy surrounding it. The blog site revealed how many were looking for him in what seemed a hopelessly vast area. "Missing" posters were left at trailheads, ranger stations and hiking shops. And most curiously, his friends wrote convincingly that he must be still alive.

The mystery deepened. No clues to Winston's whereabouts were discovered over the winter. That was unusual for cases like his. I found myself becoming more interested in learning the details of his life. He was a cafe owner/operator, an extreme skier and mountain biker. He was an expert outdoorsman. He was a writer and philosopher.

When his body was found nine months later under mysterious circumstances I had a gut feeling that this guy had an unusual story behind him. I wanted to know what happened and what made this guy tick. The press had a field day relating the drama of this mystery, piquing interest in what happened with few real facts of his life. "Hiker Slowly Starves as he Treks Colorado's Backcountry" from the *Denver Post.* "What Happened to Winston Branko Churchill?" from *5280 Magazine.* "The Strange Saga of Winston Branko Churchill" from *Mountain Gazette.* Many compared the end of Winston's life to Christopher McCandless', as told in Jonathan Krakauer's tale *Into the Wild.*

There are certainly parallels between Churchill's strange journey and that of McCandless, but there are many more differences. Winston's story is unique. Winston was two decades older than McCandless when he died. Winston was not searching for some pie-in-the-sky lifestyle or naively approaching the mysteries of freedom and exploration of the wild. Winston was an expert outdoorsman, driven by deeply held beliefs of what is good and evil in the world.

Winston was a study in individualism and not accepting the dogma of society. Though highly intelligent, he refused to tolerate the constraints required of a college degree. He valued great life experiences rather than great wealth. He was a superior athlete who preferred individual activities that resulted in great personal reward but not trophies, money or fame. Everything he did, from non-stop mountain biking the difficult Poison Spider trail to outrageous skiing in dangerous avalanche conditions to perfecting the decorative details of his cafe by hand, he did to an intense extreme.

He refused to compromise his beliefs and green, anti-consumerist philosophy for comfort, material wealth or the almighty dollar. He was highly charismatic as well as uncompromisingly honest. He gave no excuses and asked for none. His moral code lead him successfully to a lifestyle that rewarded him with everything he wanted by the age of thirty-eight.

But a dark, ominous cloud appeared on Winston's horizon. A psychological tempest grew to consume him, leading him through a series of bewildering and frightening events that culminated in an astonishing self-annihilation within one year. Many have summarily dismissed Winston's ending by declaring he "went crazy" or "burned out on drugs" or "didn't have enough respect for Mother Nature." None of those conclusions are correct.

Winston felt deeply he had some sort of greater calling: To compel the world to live without greed, without excessive consumption, and to get back to the wilderness and find true spiritualism. The falling away from respect and connectedness to the natural world and the embracing of greed and wilderness destruction was our downfall, our original sin, our reason for the banishment from the Garden.

This philosophy was not new to Winston and neither was it unique in general. Versions of this green lifestyle have been around for decades. But what happened next was highly unusual.

Winston experienced an epiphany. He rapidly changed his life to teach the world about his philosophy. It was within our power to atone for that ancient sin and return to the Garden. He was so certain that this was the key to unlock true happiness in our culture that he was willing to put everything he had into making that change happen.

He was compelled to instigate that change, in his mind he had no choice. Not one person at a time in a grass roots movement, but the whole planet at once. He was sure it was right and he was sure he could do it. And he was an extremist. In an escalating series of actions and events, Winston would push his mind and body to the very limit of life and sanity in an attempt to overcome this insurmountable barrier of igniting a cultural upheaval, to show the world how to return to the Garden.

His story is the explosive meeting of a great cause, an impenetrable barrier to that cause, and an unstoppable will to overcome.

Winston was somewhat estranged from his family. During the last years of his life, he had many friends but only a handful who were close enough to recognize the deep changes overwhelming him. Aside from the insight of these few friends, he left behind voluminous writings that offer a window into his inner thoughts of his last days. He had written an autobiographical manuscript that he hoped to publish, and also a journal of his final days in the wilderness.

I knew Winston's story was intriguing before I read his manuscript and journal, but I was not prepared for what I saw. These works are astonishing.

They are not literary masterpieces. They contain vast tracts of trivia and uninteresting ramblings. Most who have attempted to read them lost patience and gave up. But what Winston left is a window into a mind determined and focused on an impossible task and wavering on the edge of mental collapse.

Winston lived the final months of his life in a constant psychological struggle, trying to hold himself in the center. It was as if one hand was compelled to reach into the fire of insanity while the other clasped at reality with an iron grip. His is the story of the terrible struggle of a mind pulled apart in the pursuit of a greater cause.

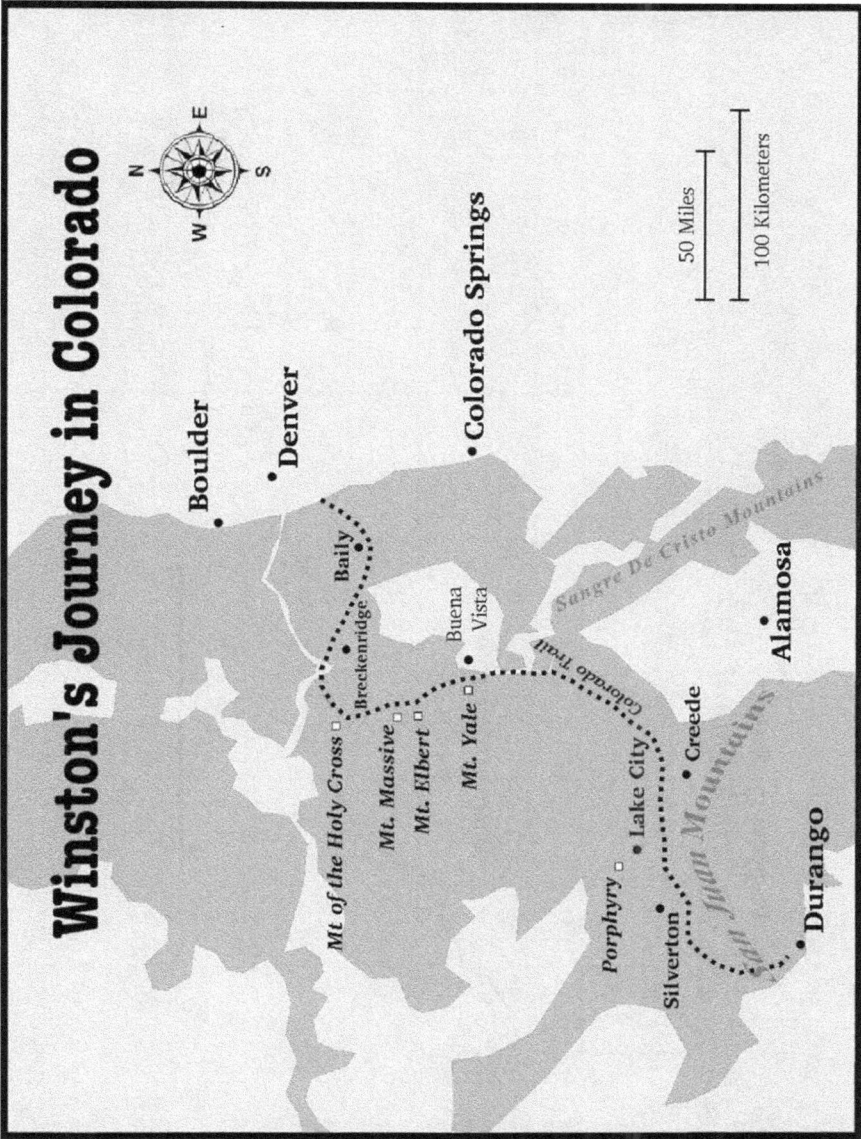

Winston's Journey in Colorado

14

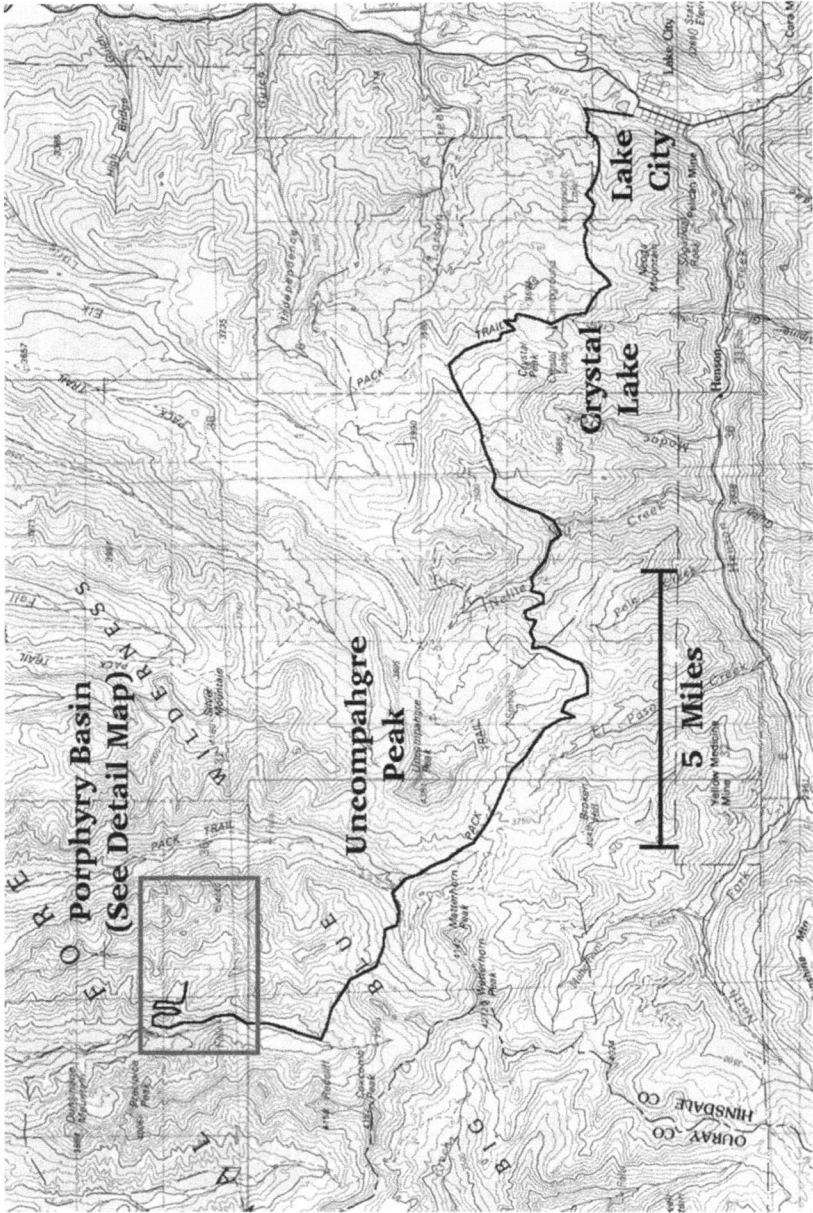

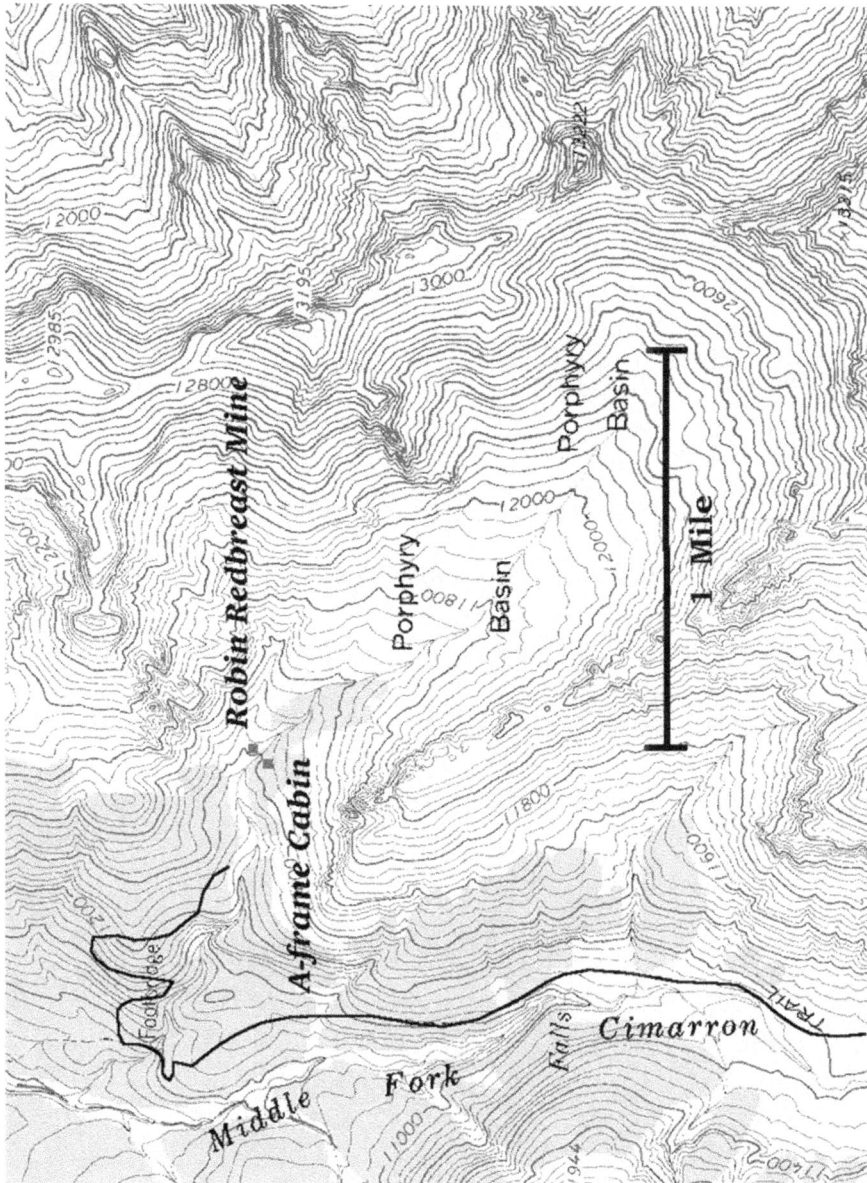

Porphyry

The moon is peeking in, her face up, and soon she'll light up my face, day turns to night, night turns to day, get wood for the fire, make sure Townshend has time to play, whatever else you do is up to you, just make sure you sleep tight and get plenty of rest, the rest just leave up to us, just keep writing to the sub-conscious mind cause we can hear you, it just might take us a little longer to figure this thing out!

Last recovered writing of W. B. C.
Colorado Trail journal
July 18, 2008

A body found in the Uncompahgre Wilderness in northern Hinsdale County on July 2 has been positively identified as Winston B. Churchill, 41, a former Silverton resident who disappeared last fall.

News brief in *The Silverton Standard*
July 9, 2009

Just before the long Independence Day weekend, two women, hiking alone in a remote high valley in a vast southwestern Colorado mountain wilderness, approached the only man-made structure they had seen since the trailhead, an empty A-frame cabin. It sat on an escarpment twenty feet above a clear, babbling creek draining snowmelt from the surrounding high peaks. They climbed up the embankment and looked for the door on the far side, facing away from the creek. As they rounded the length of the A-frame structure, the door abruptly appeared. But they were startled by an unusual object on the ground a few feet from the door.

Lying neatly before them was the mummified remains of a man in full winter clothing.

Unaware of who he might be or the circumstances of his death, the two women became upset and somewhat frightened. They were near timberline at an altitude of 11,500 feet in Porphyry Basin, a place so remote that there was no cell phone service and they had not seen another hiker on the trail for hours.

They hurriedly hiked back to the trailhead over six miles of steep, rugged terrain as the dark clouds of a thunderstorm crept over the mountains. The trail was made more challenging by jumbles of fallen pine trees, their eighteen-inch diameter trunks stacked up to three deep in places. They had to scramble around this deadfall, avoiding the sharp edges of broken branches. There was a flash of lightning followed by a deep, rumbling thunder as the storm drew near.

An hour and a half later they were back at the Middle Fork trailhead. Their car was alone in the mud parking lot next to a sign warning "NO CAMPING." They still did not have a cell phone signal. They drove north past Silver Jack reservoir over twenty-five miles of pot-holed and washboarded dirt roads to the nearest pavement.

When they finally returned to the edges of civilization, they reported their macabre finding to the Montrose county sheriff sergeant Adam Murdie. He determined that the location of body was outside his jurisdiction in Hinsdale County. Murdie phoned Hinsdale county sheriff deputy Justin Casey in Lake City. Casey brought this to the attention of Sheriff Ron Bruce. Bruce had an immediate suspicion that this might be the remains of a man reported missing the previous summer.

Lake City is an idyllic mountain village that boasts a permanent population of only 375. It is the largest town in Hinsdale County, home for nearly half the residents of what is the least populated county in the state of Colorado. It is surrounded by a thousand square miles of roadless pine forest, wild rivers, expansive lakes, deep valleys and a hundred-some mountains, six of which tower higher than 14,000 feet.

Within this expanse are three vast wilderness areas, the Uncompahgre, the La Garita, and the Weminuche. The Weminuche wilderness alone encompasses more than a half million acres, it is so large and free of human intervention that a reported sighting of a Grizzly bear were given credence, a majestic animal long thought to be extinct within the borders of the state.

Though appearing on a map as independent swaths of land, these three wilderness areas are the most primitive, natural and minimally disturbed environments of the vast Uncompaghre National Forest. This is the legendary Colorado romanticized in stories and songs. A limitless sea of mountains and forest where the air is crisp and blue, the sun intense and the stars countless, and winter snow so deep that it can bury an entire house.

Winston had been missing in these wildlands since September 2008. He was last seen in Lake City. The Hinsdale county sheriff's department was very familiar with the Churchill case, having conducted a massive months-long search involving scores of people.

It was soon determined that the body found by the two women was indeed the remains of Winston. An autopsy revealed startling facts. Churchill had died of malnutrition and exposure. He had starved to death under the frozen sky of a mountain winter. His time of death was estimated to be in late November or early December 2008. This was several months after he had vanished. He was still alive while searchers tried in vain to find him.

Called "Bronco" by his family, he has become infamous in his inexplicable demise. Speculation arose that he was unprepared for the conditions, that he was a drug freak or a lunatic. This is certain: Bronco was an expert outdoorsman, he was an extreme athlete, charismatic, highly intelligent, and prone to obsession for a cause. He was an adventurer who constantly tested the limits of his body and mind, challenged the wild and the dangerous edges of his consciousness and awareness.

He was a businessman, owner and proprietor of the hip Mobius Cycles and Cafe in Silverton. He was an extreme snowboarder and mountain biker. He was a philosopher, always examining the meaning and values of life. He was an author, having feverishly written a nearly five hundred page manuscript in a matter of months. He had dozens of friends, many of whom loved and venerated him.

Yet he met his demise in one of the most unpredictable, bizarre and tragic manners possible, in an attempt to find God, alone and without food in a remote wilderness. The last year of his life witnessed the startling transformation of Winston from athlete and businessman to wandering ascetic willing to die for a cause.

Mobius

When I first opened up Mobius Cycles & Café the locals would often ask me whether I was in it for the long haul, or if I was just passing through. I would tell them that I planned on dying there; it was my own little joke.

W. B. C.

Spring, 2005. Silverton, Colorado. By any measure of success you care to use, Winston had made it. He had just attained a goal that many others only dream about, establishing an ideal business in a perfect location of Silverton, Colorado. He had high hopes that Mobius Cycles and Cafe would earn the reputation of serving the best mocha in southwest Colorado, as well as become the go-to shop for bike repairs for those extreme summer single-track riders exploring the rugged wildlands just outside of town.

The combo coffee house and mountain bike repair shop was located at 1309 Greene Street. It was next door to the Silverton brewpub and across the street from an outdoor gear shop on the main drag of a town of less than two-dozen streets. Originally settled during the mining boom of the late 1800s, Silverton's current population of around seven hundred permanent residents have survived on mountain tourism.

Located at the convergence of four valleys, the town sits at a breathless 9,300 feet above sea level, and this is the low point of the area. Surrounding the town on every side are rugged, steep triangular mountains rising to over 13,000 feet, their naked summits piercing the sky well above timberline.

Climbers and mountain bikers explore and ride the trails in summer. In winter, backcountry skiers challenge the slopes, many of which are so steep that natural avalanches roar down on a daily and sometime hourly basis. Just outside of town is a commercial ski area called Silverton Mountain. It is not your normal groomed resort, it caters to the more extreme elements, going as far as to offer experienced professional ski guides to lead clients through the steep and deep and to avoid avalanches.

Silverton is a paradise for those outdoor enthusiasts bent on tasting the more extreme side, something Winston was all about. He was a brash 38-year-old blessed with handsome, chiseled features and intelligent, penetrating blue eyes. His five-foot, eleven-inch frame weighed in at a muscular one hundred and fifty pounds. Topped off with shoulder-length brown hair, he had the appearance of a movie star or Olympic athlete. He had the looks women swoon over and men begrudgingly admire. His physique was honed over a life of extreme endurance sports and activities in the place he loved most, the high mountains.

Winston was recognized as a talented athlete while in his early teens. He won a highly competitive golf tournament before he knew the rules of the game. He was an early adopter of snowboarding, running a school for it at a northeastern ski resort

Opening day.

Winston prepping for a high altitude vertical snowboard descent, above. Mountain biking in Utah, below.

long before it became nationally popular. He was always leading the pack on extreme mountain bike routes and challenged the steepest and most dangerous snow slopes on skis.

He would hike in the wilderness for twelve hour stretches nonstop. Despite athletic abilities that nearly always put him in front of everyone, he did not let his ego get the best of him.

Winston was also gifted with an engaging intelligence. He would constantly challenge his friends with a new, esoteric idea. He loved philosophic discussions and always sought out the truth. He would ask "Have you ever contemplated a Mobius strip? Have you thought about our origins? Do we understand the hidden consequences of the Middle Eastern wars and environmental destruction in the name of greed?"

Winston vigorously embraced honesty in a world he felt was built on half-truths and deception. He despised dishonest ideas and dishonest people to a fault and refused to play politics. "He could be an asshole if he thought you weren't genuine," explained one friend. His honesty was a bit too brutal for many of the difficult relationships necessary in life, such as between a boss and his employee, and had caused Winston a certain amount of suffering, but it also earned him friends who were deeply loyal, and he returned that loyalty.

Most of the time, however, Winston was unusually friendly and charismatic, and he had a deep empathy for the underdog. Because he himself had struggled with poverty for much of his childhood, he understood the difficulties some had of acquiring even the basics. His economic struggles did not make him lust for luxuries but instead had the profound effect of instilling compassion for others in similar situations.

"He was always super generous," Jonathan Wrobel recalled. "For instance, there were the small things like this time we were in a grocery store and an Hispanic woman was in line with her young child trying to pay for grapes. She was embarrassed that she didn't have enough cash for them. Winston immediately stepped up and paid for them without a second thought."

Jonathan was one of Winston's closest friends. They had met in 2001 in a Denver park where Jonathan and his girlfriend were walking their dog. Winston, who was out playing with his own dog, Townshend, struck up a conversation with Jonathan's girlfriend. Jonathan's immediate reaction was, Hey! Who's this guy trying to pick up my girl? But after they all started talking together, Jonathan began to relate to Winston.

"People tend to connect in certain ways. I was the open, sensitive guy and Winston was reclusive but the epitome of cool. He was really authentic and true to himself. At the time, Winston was working as a general manager at Turin Bicycles in Denver, a high-end bicycle sales and service shop. Everyone liked him there and he had a passion for his work. He was a genuine nice guy. He would always fix Gilbert's bike for free. Gilbert was a developmentally disabled customer who would hang out around Turin's."

Both Jonathan and Winston had a passion for the wilderness and outdoor sports. Over time they would bike, snowboard, hike and explore the Colorado mountains together. Jonathan was always impressed by Winston's athletic ability, his intellectual prowess and his purity of mind. "He was good at everything he did and absolutely meticulous. He would ride with pro and semi-pro mountain bikers and would kick their ass. He decorated his condo down to the last detail, including a doorknob made of rock. Who thinks of that stuff?"

Jonathan acknowledged that for all his talents and intellect, it was unlikely Winston would get far in the business world filled with marketing, negotiating and politics. "He had a hard time believing in rhetoric, politics and bullshit. I am manager at REI, Inc., I understand that I have to play the game, but Winston couldn't figure out how to fit into it."

He could be his own man in Silverton, though, serving customers in his cafe and answering only to himself. If need be, he could escape the grind by hanging a "gone skiing" sign on his front window and swoosh over to the snow-capped peaks just beyond his doorstep. Winston worked hard and made that dream a reality.

"After he bought the coffee shop he pretty much gutted it and rebuilt everything," Shanna Rivera explained. "He built the bar and the furniture, everything." Shanna had been Winston's live-in girlfriend starting in the mid-1990s but had broken it off years before Winston opened his cafe. She had re-connected with him during the period he was in Silverton. "I hadn't heard from him for a couple years and then I got a package containing a cup embossed with the words 'Mobius Cycles and Cafe'. That's how I found out he had opened a cafe."

The ambigram logo for Mobius Cycles and Café.

The two had met ten years before at the home of a mutual friend in Denver. She was impressed. "It was difficult to explain him, he was smart had a way with words, he was intense," she said. "There was no one like him." Winston had become infatuated with Shanna, the tall, dark haired woman with soft features and a wry smile, despite a significant age difference between them. She was seventeen at the time and Winston was ten years her senior. Winston had never dated a woman so much younger than himself, but they were able to work through the difficulties they encountered and eventually established a long-term relationship.

The couple moved to San Francisco in 1996 at a time when Winston was hoping to become more active in the music entertainment industry. Their endeavor lasted little more than a year before they journeyed back to Denver. At that point Shanna decided that she wanted her life to take a different direction.

"I was with him for six years and I still loved him, but when we moved back to Denver it was difficult." The friction increased as Shanna longed for a more conventional life, a life that Winston was unable to embrace.

"We would have arguments, but later he would always apologize and make me my favorite tea." Winston became more distant after their stint in California though they always felt a mental connection. "We felt we understood each other on a deep level, but he wasn't as affectionate as I needed. I wanted a boyfriend, not just a companion, though we always loved each other very much," she remembered.

Shanna added, "I might want to have a nice car or house, and that wasn't what Winston was about." In fact, Winston had the opposite desires. He was dead set against any hint of wealth, especially items that had even just a hint of luxury and status. He was anti-consumerism.

This isn't to say he thought it better to take a vow of poverty. He was not against modest needs and wants, he was not against every type of consumerism. What he did not like was the wastefulness and rampant greed praised in our society.

It was his deeply held, driving belief. He was disturbed by what he saw as the obsessive pursuit of money and "things" such as expensive cars and mansions, gaudy jewelry, stylish clothing, et cetera, in our culture.

Winston was absolutely convinced that happiness came from a more spiritual place, like being connected with nature. Chasing the latest cool toy or status symbol resulted in a life consumed by being subservient to an economic master. He felt that as a culture we would only survive by sharing, caring for each other and preserving natural resources, and the lust of acquiring vast personal wealth would destroy the world.

But in 2005, Winston the Businessman was living his ideal; to earn a modest living and enjoy what life had to offer. He spent his free time biking or boarding. He found Silverton to be perfect for both his vocation and his play. Mobius was drawing in the tourists and for the locals it was becoming the philosophical discussion center of town, something he relished. His customers would gather and talk about what really mattered in life, such as why are we here and what have we discovered that makes life worth living?

Over the next two years Winston continued to perfect Mobius. He sampled numerous roasts of coffee to serve the perfect choice. His hand crafted wooden bar and ornaments lining the shop made an impression on every visitor. He had local artists hang their paintings on his walls. Music was in the air as his business grew to the point at which in January 2007, Mobius got a mention in the New York Times travel section. He had made it.

So it was surprising to everyone that just ten months after his New York Times endorsement, the cafe was closed for business.

"I strangled Mobius," he wrote.

Winston brewing up during better times in Mobius

Roots

This is not a single-use disposable Planet.
And We are not single-use disposable People.

W. B. C.

1970s, Wandering in the Western Wilderness. Winston did not begin life at the front of the pack. He lived most of his childhood in poverty.

His father, also named Winston Churchill, was an enlisted man in the U.S. Army serving duty in Germany when in 1964 he met Mirjana, a Serbian woman who had fled her homeland as a child refugee during World War II. Winston, Sr. and Mirjana, who already had a daughter Jovanka, fell in love and were soon married. Their first child together was Winston, Jr., followed by Robert, both born in Germany.

A couple of years later, Churchill was stationed at Key West, Florida, and moved his family with him. Despite the idyllic setting at the edge of the tropical Caribbean, their marriage did not survive the move and soon Winston Sr. and Mirjana divorced. Winston Jr. was seven years old. His sister

Jovanka was nine and young Robert five. Mirjana assumed full custody of Winston and his siblings.

Life was hard for the single mother and her family. Mirjana regularly uprooted them over the next few years while chasing minimum wage jobs as a waitress or bartender. From Key West they relocated to Seattle, then to San Francisco, New Orleans and Colorado Springs. Mirjana found it difficult to earn living wages for a family of four, so she supplemented her meager income with welfare and food stamps. Through hard work and government assistance, she was at least able to put food on the table and a roof over the heads of her children.

In San Francisco, they were so destitute that they lived in a homeless shelter for six months. In Colorado Springs, they lived in welfare housing just down the street from the glitzy Broadmoor, one of the most lavish resort hotels in the city surrounded by the mansions of multi-millionaires. Throughout their childhood all three children experienced the trials and upheavals of frequently leaving familiar surroundings and established friendships, and the grind of life in poverty right next door to wealthy society in clear, glittering view.

During those years of struggle to raise a young family as a single mother, Mirjana was also determined to begin an academic career that would eventually lead to a doctorate in Sociology. She exhibited extraordinary drive and discipline to pull this off successfully. Not many would choose such a difficult path, a trait she would pass on to her children.

As an adult, Winston "...didn't want to have anything to do with money," Jovanka Mersman said of her brother. "He wanted to get people away from consumerism, he wanted everyone to get away into the wilderness" - a place where they would reconnect with their true spiritual roots. Jovanka's path in life was very different from her brother's, and though they loved and respected each other, neither could understand what motivated the other.

Jovanka shared the same background of poverty in her adolescent and teen years but has no issues with modest wealth. She is married to Dennis Mersman and they have raised three children. They have professional careers, practice a mainstream religion, and live in an upper-middle class suburb of Colorado Springs, Colorado. Both value the rewards earned from honest work.

Growing up in poverty, on the other hand, seared a different impression on young Winston's mind. An intelligent and outgoing boy, he expressed friendliness and social adeptness, and physical energy that surpassed all his friends. Despite his poverty and lack of roots, he had fun and appeared to be genuinely happy. The foundations of his later beliefs began at this time. He felt "normal" being poor, but what made some people rich? Was it fair? Why can't people be happy without wealth?

Of course Winston understood early on that he did need to earn some sort of living. For most of his life he earned what little he needed to live as a bicycle shop manager or repairman. Mobius had been the best bet at being his own man and living close to the life he desired, so it was a mystery as to why Winston killed his business. Instead of hiring someone to run it or perhaps selling it, or even closing down in an orderly manner, Winston chose the path of bankruptcy.

Jovanka, who was experienced in the operations of small businesses, had strongly encouraged an orderly dismantling so that he could start with a clean slate on any future projects. "But it was a strange bankruptcy," Jovanka revealed. "He really didn't owe much money at all. I don't know why he gave it up."

It was a whimpering end to his seemingly greatest material and lifestyle success he had ever enjoyed. It was an enterprise most people in his position would never begin, let alone intentionally kill.

Mobius would likely have supported him indefinitely. But something changed in him. It was not that he simply lost interest, but that he experienced some sort of personal discovery. He was never satisfied with the steady state activities of life, he needed to seek the non-linear transitions, the edges of existence. And he felt driven to find freedom from what he viewed as the tedium of running a business. It was, as he described, "strangling his creativity."

Winston ignored the basic fact that his modest business was allowing him to live in his beloved outdoor playground unencumbered by a nine-to-five workshop job, to continue to provide the community a philosophical clubroom, and still earn an adequate income. In essence, he ignored the fact that Mobius was keeping him alive. Not alive in the basic sense of providing food and shelter, but of also of feeding his soul, allowing him to live in his playground and be his own man at work.

But there were problems as well. The tedious minutia of running a small business, ordering coffee, cleaning the bar, washing dishes, machine maintenance, overwhelmed the positive side of the business. He was never in it for the money, but dropping out now would mean starting over once more from almost nothing and at the age of forty, he had no prospects. If this bothered him, he revealed no hint of it to anyone.

In concert with his desire for a less mundane existence, he felt he needed to do something more important, something that would impact society. He was hidden away in a small town and needed to gain a larger voice, to cry out about something that had been growing in him. He wanted to warn the world about what he felt was its coming destruction.

Over the years he had become increasingly mystified by the inequity of wealth. He would ask himself, why did a few live in extravagance while others scratched out a meager existence? And above all else, why was our culture hell-bent on striving for material gain, seemingly as the sole purpose in life? This would lead to disaster. And soon, very soon.

He knew what really mattered, it was connecting with Mother Earth, becoming one with nature, loving your neighbor, sharing the earth's resources with everyone. Consumerism was robbing people of happiness, it was obliterating countless victims in oil wars and destroying the planet. What difference did Mobius make in such a world?

He contemplated in his writing:

We can't hide from our actions, or the things we do in, or the things we do to this world, either spiritually or physically, you can never hide from them, because you're constructed from them, we all are. Everything you put out, you become; you are what your feed yourself. Flow in equals flow out... Overall, we as a collective, control the balance of the two, by what we as individuals put into that collective. Greed, hatred, and selfish actions for personal gain or power are brought to bear in the physical as well as mental maladies that affect us all. You can build a fence around it, contain it, and try and separate yourself from it if you like, as long as you understand that you're the one who created it. They are a result of everyone's actions, and you should never be able to hide from it, you should be reminded of it every time you see the diseased, the poor, the sick, or the imbalanced, whether it be people, animals, trees, land, clouds or water; it should be a reminder...

...You know those people who give those speeches? The ones who try and teach you how to help yourself and how to become more successful, you know those people. They have TV shows and books, and they go on their tours. They're like those evangelical preachers. There's not a whole lot of difference I don't think. Well, I want to do

the same thing, except with a slightly different twist. I want to go out there and tell people not to be successful. Instead I want to get them to help and rip the wheels out of the machine, and the belts, and the chains, and all that infrastructure, just tear it out of there. So it's just an empty skeleton, which is what they don't understand. That's what they are. They're an important part, because they house it, and maybe organize it, and contain it. They do their job. They have a job to do. But they don't value all those little working parts, and pieces. And without them, they don't have anything. They have the empty skeleton of industry. It's worthless. So they have to understand that. Somebody needs to bring that to their attention, somewhere in there they already do understand it, but they're too busy watching the numbers roll over in their bank accounts, to be bothered with the insignificant things, like people's lives, and shit like that. Who's got time for that?

Winston gave up on the consumer machine and began to rail against it. He embraced nature and the connectedness of all the living. And he embraced poverty.

By his early teen years Winston had developed into an insolent, trouble-making boy and his mother, already overwhelmed, was finding it impossible to handle him. She sent him to live with his father Winston Sr., once a drill sergeant but now retired from the military. Young Winston moved to New Hampshire where his situation improved significantly.

In stark contrast to his mother's economic situation at the edge of poverty, his father was living an upper middle-class life with all its trappings. Winston attended a private school and spent his free time in the pool at the Plausawa Valley Country Club while his father played rounds of golf.

Winston's natural athletic abilities earned him a junior golf tournament championship but, he admitted, he "had no respect" for the country club lifestyle. To him, it was spiritually empty. Winston wrote about the devious satisfaction he and a friend felt late one night as they stole a golf cart and spun donuts to ruin some of the greens. It was perhaps a subconscious effort to strike back at what he saw as the exorbitant wastefulness of the wealthy.

By the time Winston was in his mid-teenage years, he had not only experienced both ends of the economic spectrum but had made a decision as to which lifestyle had more purity. He had not completely accepted a life of poverty at his young age, but saw it as being more honest. His friends and family who lived in poverty were no less deserving than the wealthy. And those friends seemed more real to him, living life closer to what it actually was rather than being shielded from it by a wall of wealth.

He could also see that wealth was a distraction from what really mattered in life, namely the experience of life itself. A lifetime spent accumulating money meant a lifetime of missing out on love, fun, exploration, and play. It meant missing out on happiness. Winston was never able to relate to those who made it their highest goal to accumulate money and status.

But he was most deeply impressed by the lack of equality that wealth generated. He could not reconcile the capricious nature of who is selected to have and have not. He saw many who had wealth as ungrateful, and many who were poor as far more deserving. To him this was an inherent injustice in the world.

It was an unusual insight reasoned at an age when most boys are obsessed with rock music, video games, football and girls. His bias against wealth would grow over the years and become reinforced by his love for life experience over money.

Winston struck out on his own at the age of eighteen and soon discovered what would be lifelong passions, snowboarding and mountain biking. He moved to Lincoln, New Hampshire and rode the slopes when he wasn't operating a lift at Loon Mountain Ski Area. Over the next few years Winston eked out a living in construction, odd ski resort jobs, and bike repair shops. Eventually his talents led him to become the director and head racing coach of the Snowboarding school at Loon Mountain.

Snowboard racing.

But he had no ambition to "move up" in the working world. He established a philosophy during this period of his life that a job was simply a means of survival as he fed and refined what was important, and that was to experience of life itself. To him this would manifest as snowboarding, skiing, and mountain biking and simply being outside in the wild. He spent as much time as possible hiking and camping.

In 1993, at the age of twenty-six, he ventured to Boulder, Colorado, and began work at the bike shops around town. This is about the time he discovered his passion for music and dancing, to him another visceral experience of life itself. He immersed himself to the point that he became a disk jockey, or DJ, for private parties. He invented the stage name "DJ Verifine" and hired himself out whenever he could.

Winston amassed several crates of vinyl albums and worked the rave circuit. He was infatuated with the loud hypnotic beat, the rhythms of the body movement, and the sexy women strutting and swaying on the dance floor. He approached his music mixes as an artist approaches a masterpiece painting, as a meticulous, emotionally expressive creation from the heart, given by him for the world to experience. As he was becoming popular in the rave scene, Winston met Shanna and soon they moved to California to see how far he could go in the entertainment business.

"We moved to the Bay area in 1996 so that Winston could DJ in San Francisco. We stayed with a friend until we could move to our own place in Daly City. He was very popular." But the money wasn't enough to support the two in such an expensive locale, so Winston took a job repairing bikes at Start to Finish, a bike shop in San Francisco. "The shop was about twenty miles from our place in Daly City and Winston would always ride his bike to work and back every day."

Like most of the entertainment industry, the big money is skewed toward the top of the pyramid. A handful of the most popular DJs can make a living at it, but the vast majority struggle to make a few bucks. Shanna suggested that Winston find a promoter. She knew he was good and all he needed was publicity. But he wouldn't do it.

"He hated the idea of playing 'the game.' He thought people should recognize how good his music was on its own merits, but he made very little money," Shanna said. To Winston, the politics and marketing of his talent would taint the purity of what he considered his artistry. He could not reconcile these two. Unfortunately, only under the rarest of circumstances does anyone become a popular entertainer with no promotion at all.

DJ Verifine.

Not surprisingly, his DJing career hit a wall and his opportunities faded. In less than two years, Winston and Shanna had moved back to Colorado and subsequently went their separate ways. But the side effects of his DJing produced several twists in his life. It was inevitable that as DJ Verifine, he would come into contact with the drug MDMA, known by its street name "Ecstasy." Its ability to induce euphoria, diminish anxiety and amplify a feeling of intimacy with others makes

Ecstasy the drug of choice in the rave crowd, and it's impossible for the DJ, at the center of his audience's attention, to ignore this.

Winston experimented with Ecstasy, but by the accounts of his friends and his own admissions, it was not something that he did often. As a matter of fact, he did not really enjoy the drug. He did not like the effect it had on his mind. Winston was not prone to use, and actually had a distinct distaste for mind-numbing drugs that produced a false euphoria such as Ecstasy. But he was well aware of its popularity among his social group. DJing and performing bicycle maintenance were barely earning him a living wage. He saw an opportunity to shore up his bank account.

In 1998, Winston attempted to make a quick buck by selling a batch of MDMA pills. In an amateurish move that plainly showed he was not a professional drug dealer, Winston had a friend ship five hundred pills to his address in Boulder. Shortly after his package arrived, the cops busted through his door with guns drawn, kneed him face down on the floor, cuffed and hauled him to jail. His sentence of four years probation was effective in keeping him from ever attempting to flaunt the law in this way again.

He had put these experiences far behind him by the time he opened up Mobius in 2005. Though the next two years of his life in Silverton was not a typical nine-to-five pace, it was far more conventional than he'd ever experienced. Or wanted. He had to move on.

American Ascetic

"Our enormously productive economy demands that we make consumption our way of life, that we convert the buying and use of goods into rituals, that we seek our spiritual satisfactions, our ego satisfactions, in consumption. The measure of social status, of social acceptance, of prestige, is now to be found in our consumptive patterns. The very meaning and significance of our lives today expressed in consumptive terms. The greater the pressures upon the individual to conform to safe and accepted social standards, the more does he tend to express his aspirations and his individuality in terms of what he wears, drives, eats - his home, his car, his pattern of food serving, his hobbies.

...We need things consumed, burned up, worn out, replaced, and discarded at an ever-increasing pace. We need to have people eat, drink, dress, ride, live, with ever more complicated and, therefore, constantly more expensive consumption."

Economist Victor Lebow, *The Real Meaning of Consumer Demand*
Journal of Retailing
Spring 1955

The demise of Mobius Cycles and Cafe signaled the end of Winston's experiment with the machinery of capitalism. He could not reconcile the business side with his philosophy of embracing nature, anti-consumerism and caring for one's neighbor. Running a business was, at best, an obstacle to his higher goals and at worst a detriment, an enemy to those goals.

To be honest, Winston did play the game of material acquisition to a degree. Besides his business, he possessed an expensive mountain bike, a truck, and had taken out a mortgage on a condo. It could be argued that he was well on the road to the same consumerism that obsesses our culture. More to the truth of the matter is that our culture enables us to believe that an automobile and house ownership are necessities and we should own them before even thinking about the implications of ownership.

Winston was not immune to this trap, but he never thought his possessions would lead to happiness. To him they were merely practical tools to get through life. The Mobius experiment transformed his view even further until he concluded essentially all consumerism is in vain and that happiness and fulfillment must come from within.

By renouncing the pursuit of wealth and embracing the path of compassion and caring for nature and people, Winston chose the path of asceticism. Though he never literally declared "I am now an ascetic," he became a de facto ascetic by his philosophy and new lifestyle.

The dictionary defines an ascetic as someone who dedicates their life to the pursuit of an ideal of high morals or ethics. A major aspect of this life is self-denial of both material and pleasurable experiences. Some ascetics induce greater suffering on themselves by avoiding earthly pleasure and indulgence.

The life of an ascetic is well outside of the norm, especially in a wealthy culture where even the poorest among us has a myriad of pleasurable experiences in which to indulge. An ascetic from a poor family in India may be giving up the assurance of a bland meal a day. His family may have lived in a crowded hovel without electricity, no internet, TV, or phone, no indoor plumbing and had to haul water long distances just to survive. In that world the switch from normal life to that of an ascetic is vastly different than that in a Western culture.

The ascetic lifestyle in Indian culture is very much accepted today as it has been for thousands of years as a reasonable choice in life. As a matter of fact, it is accepted and encouraged to some degree all over Asia. Ascetic lifestyles are deeply tied to religious beliefs and those ties are key to their cultural respect.

But self-denial in the Western culture of vast material wealth is so "out there" as to seem pathological. In a culture whose most powerful symbols are of wealth and status, there is little room for the austere lifestyle not singularly focused on making as much money possible. An ascetic may gain approval and even granted high praise if they have dedicated their life to working for a noble charity or for some higher principle or moral, but only if it is absolutely selfless dedication to this narrow definition.

So if an ascetic doesn't choose calling such as becoming a religious monk or a volunteer caregiver at a hospice for terminally ill children, their life is generally looked down upon as wasting the resources of society, as if we can't afford a very poor man in our midst as we wallow in our comparatively vast wealth. They are considered lazy freeloaders because they do not have jobs, as if we were all beasts of burden whose primary function is to slave for the machinery of consumerism.

To become an ascetic in our culture one must endure the deprived lifestyle on top of the risk of being shunned by society. So why do it? Is it a mental illness? The truth is, an ascetic believes that giving up wealth and pleasurable experiences allows them greater freedom and connection to spirituality, peace of mind and clarity of thought. This is almost the definition of happiness. Attachment to toys, status and pleasure is a great distraction, just as an addict believes his drug of choice leads to bliss when in fact it destroys him.

Acquiring more money does not free one from work; it likely results in the recursive need for more work and responsibility. Indulging in sex, delicious meals and intoxicating drugs and alcohol is fleeting and results in no long term peace of mind or contentment, but many times to just the opposite as we strive ever to reproduce the pleasurable feelings after they evaporate.

Status and expensive things are addicting but certainly not fulfilling as one seeks ever more without end. The basic desire for these can never be fulfilled.

Winston understood this and it was his reason for choosing the path of asceticism. Though in a small minority, Winston wasn't alone in this belief. Other modern day non-religious ascetics have made this lifestyle choice as well. A few have made it their duty to expound on the beneficial aspects of their philosophies for all to see.

Boulder, Colorado, where Winston spent many years of his life, is a town that almost defies explanation. Located in one of the most picturesque valleys at the base of the Front Range northwest of Denver, this relatively small city is home to the University of Colorado, several federally funded and operated high tech research labs, scores of outdoor recreation-oriented business headquarters, and a myriad of high tech and biotech firms.

Not to be outdone on either the intellectual or athletic fronts, Boulder is the home of three Nobel prize winners and dozens of Olympic medalists, not bad for a town of just over one hundred thousand residents. Fantastic year-round weather and easy access to the mountains attracts world-class runners, bikers, skiers, and rock and ice climbers. Boulder can boast of one of the most highly educated populations in the nation.

Living in Boulder comes at a steep price. The cost of housing in the city is on par with that of the most expensive towns in the United States. Fortunes are made and spent in this city. But in parallel to all the wealth and status on prominent display is a large homeless population, as witnessed by those who "fly a sign" on street corners begging for money. There seems to be at least one transient holding out a cardboard sign begging for a handout on every busy street corner in town.

Alcoholism, drug addiction, mental illness, being forced out of, or simply giving up on the rat race, are skid-row stories as numerous as those who live on the street. There are some, however, that do not fall into these categories but have chosen a lifestyle of extreme poverty - they have become ascetics. Max Weller is one of them.

Weller has his own opinion as to why Boulder is the host to a disproportionate number of transients. "Most of the transients begging on the street corners ride the bus here from Denver. Boulder is a party town. Along with cheap booze, they know there are plenty of drugs available," he explains.

Weller is quick to point out that not all of the homeless are partying beggars. "Most of them [homeless] are normal folk struggling to get back on their feet. Unfortunately, the people with the highest profile are the alcoholics or drug abusers just looking to beg money for a party."

"The people of Boulder are very generous. There are many resources here for the homeless including meals, day services at the [homeless] shelter such as showers with free soap, lockers and free use of a phone. Medical services at the People's Clinic. It makes me angry when these guys waltz in here with the attitude that Boulder owes them a living, not to mention a place to party."

Max knows this culture well, he has been living on the streets of Boulder since 2007. But he defies the stereotype. He does not drink or use drugs. He has never "feigned mental illness to receive a 'crazy check'," referring to the monthly Social Security Disability Income checks that many transients in Boulder receive, in his opinion fraudulently, and then used to pay for a week in a cheap hotel room with plenty of booze and/or drugs.

Max camps out most of the year. He stays in the Boulder Shelter for the Homeless on the coldest nights when it might dip well below zero degrees Fahrenheit, but in general he will camp out in all weather including rain and snow. Max has been living this way for four years.

"I love the freedom of being alone at night, sleeping under the stars in summer or even under a heavy-duty tarp with snow falling in winter. It's a sort of total relaxation for me, both physical and emotional," he told me of his current life. It wasn't always like that for him.

Years ago Max had a conventional lifestyle. "I've not only been a family farmer and a farmhand or ranch hand working for others, I was a city councilman in my hometown, a retail firearms dealer and gunsmith, a bank security officer, and an activist in the politics of my hometown as a private citizen."

But a decade ago Max's life began to unravel. The first blow was the death of his older brother, someone he had felt very close to and assumed the role of his "surrogate dad," his father having died when Max was only four. Then his uncle contracted a "catastrophic illness," precipitating the loss of the family farm, of which Max was part owner, due to the exorbitant medical expenses. His mother then became deathly ill, and she began to spend her life savings on medical expenses. Already a drinker, Max's alcoholism worsened.

Then his mother died. Her medical expenses drained not only all of her assets, but also all of Max's life savings. He was dead broke, alcoholic, and depressed. He had no real prospects and still needed to make mortgage payments. In desperation, he "became a white collar criminal" and began forging his mother's signature on her Social Security checks that continued to come in after her death.

"My ill-gotten gains weren't even sufficient to keep up with utility bills and property taxes, however, and I became serious about suicide," Max admits. Having lost the two most beloved in his family as well as all his money, his life spun out of control and he couldn't live with himself.

His crimes were quickly discovered. He was arrested and subsequently served a five-year prison term in the Missouri State Correctional System. In an event most would view as rock bottom, Max sees his arrest and conviction as one of the most positive in his life. He even thanks the police captain of his home town for "saving his life."

He got back on track and dried out, but he also had an epiphany: Upon his release from prison, he would exist on a minimal level. "Having lost everyone and everything I once loved, I know it is my role now to live as an ascetic."

He currently lives without the complications of a conventional life. Max admits that even before he was homeless he didn't have the typical societal constraints that most have, "no wife and kids, no mortgage, no stressful career grind," but he made the choice not to ever seek them in the future. What does he feel the downside is? "The worst I suffer as an ascetic is silly people and stale bagels; the former I can move away from and the latter I feed to Br'er Fox [the fox who frequently visits his campsite]."

Max keeps busy as a blogger about issues surrounding his lifestyle. He's been blogging from public Internet connections for more than a year about issues that would never be brought up in politically correct company in Boulder. The fact that parole officers dump parolees at the Boulder Homeless Shelter. Sex offenders on parole to the shelter who continue to entice children on the public bus or at the library. Pretentious city council members. And the perplexing lack of common sense invariably exhibited by "Boulder Ph. D." types, a sarcastic jab at one of the most educated cities in America.

Max is articulate, clean, sane, sober and capable of living a conventional life. I asked him why he opted out.

"To wax poetic, I feel a oneness with something much greater than myself, although I really can't give it a precise name. I have no plans at present to change my lifestyle. It could stand some minor improvements, of course, which I'm working on. Now, after living this way for a time, I find it has its own rewards which I couldn't have guessed at before," Max told me.

The conventional lifestyle that Max was essentially forced out of precipitated the best outcome he could imagine. He simply let go of his material attachments. This is exactly the thinking that Winston advocated and eventually chose for himself as well.

There is a more famous, radical and long-term example of this anti-consumerism lifestyle from another former Boulder resident now living on the edge of society.

Daniel Suelo, originally Daniel Shellabarger, is a 50-something year old hermit who spends his time living in a cave near Moab, Utah. He has refused to use money since autumn 2000. He does not earn money and does not accept it. If anyone gives him cash, he will not spend it, immediately giving it away.

Like Weller and other numerous transients of America, Suelo is homeless and does not hold a job. Suelo is highly educated (has a college degree), and also like Weller, does not have an alcohol or drug problem and has no discernible mental illness. He is clean, healthy, and as several friends and acquaintances testify, one of the happiest people around.

Suelo's secret to survival is to live off the refuse of society. To be specific, the trash of Moab. In what is thrown away in this small town, he has found good clothing, shoes, cooking utensils, and reading material. He gets garbage food from grocery stores and claims he has never gotten ill from contamination. He has precious few possessions and quite frankly couldn't have or use any more in his fifteen by five foot secret cave in the wilderness.

Suelo, like Weller, also blogs about his philosophy using the free computers in the library and has gained a bit of notoriety in the press. "Addiction to money fuels corruption", he told a *Denver Post* reporter, and that he realized "...we all possess nothing, [which] is the cornerstone of all spiritual endeavors and religions."

Suelo's early life gave no hint as to where he would wind up today. He graduated from the University of Colorado with a degree in Anthropology. He then went on to serve two years in the Peace Corps in Ecuador, returning to Boulder to work in the homeless shelter and battered woman's shelter.

These jobs did not generate the income needed to match his living expenses of rent, car payment, credit card payments, groceries, gas, and all the little necessities of conventional life. In reaction to a growing despair, he decided he did not need his "stuff." He gave it all away.

He concluded that money sapped the energy of society. The want, chasing, and management of money to acquire material possessions that were, in his opinion, unnecessary in the first place.

He gave up the idea of ownership or living in a conventional shelter. He does not deal with money at all, nor will he trade work for anything material. He considers even barter, for example trading work for food, a form of money.

His reward, he says, is that he has no debts, has no material wants, and no stressful job to worry about. And he claims that there is more than enough to live on in the refuse of society. "I know that there is enough food to feed a village in one dumpster behind Wal-Mart or Sam's. All I'm taking are a few crumbs falling from this opulent table," he claims.

What Suelo does possess is a keen sense of anti-consumerism and spiritualism. He gladly shares his philosophies with others on his blog.

He is not attempting to be self-sufficient and does accept charity when he needs it, in the form of temporary shelter or a useful item, but of course never in the form of currency. Suelo is really just living a life rejecting the strong cultural currents that sweep the vast majority of us into excess consumerism.

These are the lives of American ascetics. Though the ascetic life is not suitable for most, for example, it would be extremely difficult to raise a family this way, it is an accepted lifestyle in much of the world. Suelo and Weller, like the Indian ascetics, live spiritual lives on their own terms and do not ask for handouts. The question for the rest of us is, do we have no tolerance for ascetics in our society and, in fact, tend to drive some of them into the mental abyss?

Our culture of rampant consumerism does not appear to make us happy, nor does it appear to be culturally fulfilling. Dazzling technological toys do not give us long-term satisfaction. Miraculous medical treatments extend our time but do nothing for the real quality of our lives. Expensive mansions or luxury cars do not make us wise. But they do cause us stress, to work longer hours to pay for the debts they incur.

The Sherpas of Nepal, living in the poorest communities on earth, are considered to be some of the happiest. Large segments of the population have no electricity, running water or sewers. Even the middle class Sherpas have few possessions in comparison to American middle class society.

Yet they are undeniably a happy culture as witnessed by the hundreds of thousands of annual trekkers to their villages in the Himalayas. Almost every one of those trekkers agrees, the Sherpas are sincerely happy. They credit their culture based on Buddhist beliefs for what seems to be paradoxical contentment. All the conveniences of a modern technological society are marketed to us as ways to relieve greed, stress, worry, depression and suffering but in actuality seem to make them worse.

Ascetics such as Weller, Suelo, and even Winston, are of the secular mindset. They are not religious in terms of organized religion, but holding spiritual values. Other examples of secular asceticism might include a creative person such as an artist or a writer or a musician who devotes their life to their art, forgoing a career or job that would provide a steady living income to focus on their gift. The "starving artist" might live in poverty, shacking up with friends when possible and eating meager food portions all in the name of perfecting a painting, becoming a virtuoso or writing the next great American novel.

Much as both Weller and Suelo, Winston's decision to become an ascetic was triggered by his desire to escape the soul-crushing machinery of capitalism. But that was just the beginning for Winston. He didn't know exactly where it would lead, only that he needed to change his path in life. He was certain that his anti-consumerism philosophy would be more fulfilling, lead to more contentment and satisfaction and less frustration and suffering. And like all ascetics, he began to eliminate worldly distractions.

Winston knew the ascetic lifestyle would be difficult, but he also knew he was dedicated to his cause, and he had the determination to follow through.

Rise of the Demons

...I began eliminating things from my life. I vowed to no longer work, no longer pay any bills, no longer earn or ask for money. I no longer drove my truck, I no longer had a phone, I no longer talked with anyone, isolating myself and continuously writing for 40 days.

W. B. C.

December, 2007. Lakewood, Colorado. After shuttering Mobius, Winston made the long drive between Silverton and Lakewood, a suburb of Denver, two times over the next two weeks.

He contemplated on the next phase of his life. He had a goal but no plan of action. How would he change the world? He was driving on a gravel road into a dark forest, trying to reach the other side, hoping the road would eventually open up into a green meadow and not end abruptly at a cliff face. He was sure that meadow was ahead. He was on autopilot, but certain the answer would reveal itself.

It did. An idea crystallized in Winston's mind during these long traverses across the high and lonely Colorado Mountains - a book. He would write a best seller that would chronicle his journey in life and how he arrived at his anti-consumerist, green philosophy. He would describe how he had come to understand that mankind was quickly using up the planet in its relentless drive toward ruin. It was a book that needed to be written, it was imperative that he profess to everyone what he had come to understand.

His epiphany struck at 11,230 feet while traversing Monarch Pass:

> *Now this becomes a cause... Am I willing to devote my life to getting my thoughts down, my opinions down? ...If I compromise and say, ok, I'll work a regular job, and when I get home at night, after I take my dog for a walk, maybe make some dinner, pay some bills, and then with that time that's left, I'll sit down and be creative. No. I've tried that. It doesn't work. I think one of the reasons it doesn't work, is because... this is serious stuff. This is not to be toyed with. This is not a part-time, part-part-time, occasional Sunday afternoon, and Wednesday evenings only, venture. This is big time, this is the real deal... Are you willing to sacrifice, and/or devote your life to it? Are you willing to give up everything? What you know to be everything? Your material things? Your house? Your truck? Those god-damned records? That income to buy a new toaster? And the new toaster? All those things? Are you willing to give all that up? And you're not giving it up for anything tangible...There's a possibility that I'm going to write this shit down,*

and people are going to read it and think, "This guy is a fucking loon!" ... [That is] Until someone accidentally stumbles onto my book. You're flipping through pages... Next thing you know you're reading something that sets off, some sort of chain of, an epiphany of events. And I guess, that, that's the chance I want to take. That's one of the reasons behind this and that is the only potential of anything that even resembles that of a guarantee that I have.

What would you do if you were certain that society would soon self-destruct? What if you accepted this as surely as you believe the sun will rise tomorrow? Would you keep it to yourself or would you try to warn the world? And how would you warn the world?

Prior to opening Mobius, Winston had been living in Lakewood and worked as the general manager of Turin Bicycles, a sales and repair shop located in downtown Denver. During his stint at the shop, Winston managed to scrape together enough cash to put a down payment on a condo in Lakewood. He had been renting it out during his two years in Silverton, but it was now vacant. Winston moved himself, his dog Townshend, and his few possessions back into his condo. He then set up shop to crank out a book.

Winston had never before tackled a large writing project that a book manuscript would require, but of course was never one to shy away from a challenge. In fact, he felt he had no choice. This would be his medium to warn the world of what was coming, what had been revealed to him and to teach a better way. As Winston began to obsess with writing, he removed anything from his world that might be a distraction.

He focused with laser-like intensity to illuminate his philosophies. He gave no thought to editing or publishing his work. As far as anyone knows, he never tried to sell his writing. He wrote and sent snippets to his friends and family for review. Other than the solitary goal of finishing his book, it appeared that Winston had no further plan for his life and events started to spin out of control.

He lived like a monk in a mountain cave. Solitary. Isolated. He did not have a TV or internet connection. He didn't even have a phone line. When he wasn't writing, he read voraciously or went on day-long rides and hikes. He meditated in silence for hours on end.

When he was writing, words erupted with the pent-up energy of a long dormant volcano. In the end he would produce a prodigious four hundred and ninety-five-page manuscript, completed in less than six months. More than four hundred thousand words boiled out from his mind. His process of constant writing, exercising and meditating without rest, without a break, in physical and social isolation, had a profound impact on him.

Winston the Ascetic began to explore the concept of God. He began with an intellectual rather than inspirational approach. Winston had never been a total atheist, but he was far from any sort of emotional connection with a supreme being. His inquiries did not begin with a spiritual rebirth, he was simply thinking about a concept in which he was building a new interest. But where to start?

He does not begin with interpretations of established religious thought but of his own ideas. He writes as if teaching of what God is, as if he already has some insight. In one passage he writes:

True God, will never be seen, or depicted as
a being, God is an action, God is a way of life,
God is the one who keeps on swimming, and helps

the person next to him to keep on swimming. God isn't going to command you to live your life by a certain set of rules, God wants you to find those rules yourself, God wants you to tap into that channel, and find yourself. You'll never "find" God, you can only search for eternity, and the hopes of God, is that during that search, you find everything else you need, including your path, and your purpose, as well as your own true identity. Anyone who claims to have found God; isn't looking hard enough. You don't "find" harmony, you make it, and it isn't something you make once, and place above your fireplace on a nail. You have to keep making it, and you need to make it everywhere you go; it's the dedication to that process that brings you closer to "God", but don't expect to actually get there, as a physical form. You can tap into God, and you can reach into God, but you won't become one with God, until the lights go out on your physical abode.

Despite the assertive tone of his writing, he was actually trying to understand what God "is." When taken in the context of his entire manuscript, it is obvious that this and his many other descriptions of God are really propositions, tests, and thought experiments. It is apparent that he was striving for greater understanding and writes down everything that comes to his mind, from the thoughtful descriptions above to other passages that at first seem like allegories constructed from an active imagination:

If we follow the Gods all the way back, through the furthest reaches of recorded history, we find "Anu" and his two sons "Enlil" and

"Enki". Now I think it helps, especially for those out there who don't believe in God, which I actually think is fine, don't think you need to believe in God, sometimes I wonder myself if I do, but I think it helps here if we don't take this literally. Let's say that "Anu" is "God", whatever that means to you, or whatever you want that to mean or represent. Now the two sons, we want to take out of the picture, we don't want to slowly remove this notion we have that they are sons, or that they are people, and then we want to eliminate any lingering possibility that they are "Gods" or "Sons of God", we want to give them a simple identity, and I'm sure they aren't going to mind, because this is why they're here. So unfortunately what we're going to have to do, is have one represent Good, and the other unfortunately represent evil, this is only a lesson, and will have no effect on reality. Maybe.

In ancient Sumerian mythology, which is as far back as Western cultural history has recorded, Anu was god of the heavens. He was father of Enlil, god of the air, and Enki, god of the water. Though Enlil and Enki were not considered by the ancients to be one-sided as good or evil, Winston had chosen to use this early Middle Eastern myth to begin his thought experiment about the origins of good and evil in the world.

He used accurate names and relationships from an ancient myth and builds his own understanding upon it. He does not give detailed reference to his source and clearly never claims his tale to be truthful, but uses it as a philosophical and moral allegory. It is clear that Winston knows something of religious mythology even if he hasn't had previous deeply held beliefs.

A sudden interest in understanding God was an unusual transformation for Winston. "That was the really strange thing,"

Shanna remembered. "Before that, he was not religious and really didn't talk about God much. It's strange that he wrote so much about it." Shanna had remained Winston's close friend even after they split up. Her insight into Winston's behavior was that of a long-term friend, partner and confidant. Her immediate reaction was that Winston's concern with God and spirituality was well out of the ordinary for him.

But it continued, growing over the days and weeks until it dominated nearly all his thought.

He underwent a strange sequence of events beginning in mid-December through the end of January. He tells of experiencing a sort of ecstatic "energy and crazy dreams," flashes of light and heat. He has vague feelings of a flu-like illness and notices strange breathing patterns and heart rhythms that develop spontaneously. He begins having visions of an ethereal world populated with beings of good and evil. He is perplexed at these phenomena but is completely lucid in his descriptions of it.

At the peak on the night of January 29, Winston experienced what he describes as an epic battle with demons. He wrote:

> *I remember having great difficulty in trying to fall asleep, like something was affecting my breathing, as well as my heart rate. My thoughts also seemed difficult to control, and tended to constantly stray into the darkness, as well as thinking themselves into corners, and repetitive nonsense. I would find myself working to pull out of these downward spirals, only to find myself back into another one...*
>
> *Something told me that I was in store for a great fight, with an enemy that exuded nothing but darkness and great terror.*

The battle becomes a series of mental challenges, puzzles and logic problems to "trap me into insanity that would become my very reality." Solving the problems allows him to retain his sanity, but to defeat the demons he must also perform certain "rituals." The demons attempt to trick or distract him from the rituals that he knew nothing about but were innately discovered when needed:

> ...[the puzzles] were intended to be distractions, to keep me from taking the action that I was about to take, an action that I knew nothing about, nor had ever practiced before in my life. It was as if I was tapping into something that had been taught to me without my knowing, or something I had learned in a previous life, but something positive was definitely guiding me, because I was performing these "rituals" that I knew nothing about, breathing exercises and patterns that seemed very specific. I went through a series of rituals that to me seemed specifically designed for the exorcism of such demons.
>
> ...I remember my chest constantly rising and heaving, and my head arching back, opening my throat and airway. I remember constantly laughing during my exhalations, as much as one could laugh in such a state, but it was definitely a noticeable laugh, and it was a dark laugh all my own.
>
> ...I remember towards the end of the ordeal, my head rotating around in circles, not like in The Exorcist, but more like the circular motion one might use to clean a window. I felt at one point as if I was raised up slightly and then set back down. I felt at one point the moisture condensing on my skin in tiny droplets, causing

me to feel almost electric. Each of these rituals were followed or preceded by a deep inhalation that would arch my back, as well as tilt my head back, opening my throat.

Eventually Winston feels he has defeated the demons. But then he hears a noise. The demons have emerged from his thoughts and have become physical manifestations:

...At this point in time I could hear one of the demons upstairs seemingly pulling a gun out of a drawer, and dropping it. Then I could hear him trying to load it, dropping bullets onto the floor, as he tried.

He hears a demon say "Just sleep until seven." Winston then hears the sound of keys jingling and so picks up his key ring and rattles them in his ear, "a signal for the good guys to come." Then he remembers the number "7" also means "key" and he interprets that to mean, use your key to get out the door before 7 a.m.

Realizing this is the final ritual he must perform he does just that. He leaves his condo and climbs Green Mountain, one of the foothills located just outside his home. He arrives at the summit just before 7 a.m. The sun rises above the horizon literally only minutes later. Winston "wins" the battle.

This bizarre sequence of events is echoed in an eerie manner with themes and motifs expressed throughout Winston's manuscript. The symbols and ideas of his battle with the demons are interwoven throughout his subsequent thought. Winston had previously written that Enki, pronounced "in-KEY," represents "good." He also writes in several completely unrelated passages that the number 7, also a symbol for a "key" as well as "male life force." Enki also represents male life force in the universe.

To Winston, the sun brings light and always represents good and the defeat of evil. Though he never mentions the sun or sunrise in the story of this battle, much of his later writing connects the sun with good defeating evil.

The number 7 is associated with "good," "key," and "male." Enki is "good," and "male." Demon battle won at 7 a.m. At sunrise.

The timing of the sunrise and the fact that Winston makes no mention of it is astounding. It is impossible to believe that he consciously constructed these symbols and events to align so well.

His "battle with demons" will become the major inflection point in Winston's life. It was ground zero for what was to come.

Sumerian mythology tells us that Enki's "sacred number" is forty. After the battle, Winston associated an intense spiritual meaning to the number forty (he happens to be forty years old). Winston will attach a great importance to the forty days following his battle and find his experience so profound that for the rest of his life he will call it his *awakening*.

Kundalini Awakening

You could have ten, twenty or a hundred lives go by before you age spiritually, but when you finally do, you are experiencing your spiritual awakening, the birthday of your soul. But if your life, and your soul are not progressing spiritually then that "birthday of your soul" that "Kundalini Experience" might feel more like having the flu, followed perhaps by some crazy dreams. Now throughout your life, God, or your higher self has been dishing out these little bits of guidance to you, and depending on what you do with it will dictate whether or not you get any more. God will keep handing out those doses of enlightenment until you use them the wrong way, or even if you don't use them at all. God wants to see what you can do with it, God wants to see what your true potential is, and who really knows as a society what our true potential is, we sure as hell don't.

W. B. C.

Winston had become obsessed with God.

This development would ratchet up his drive to expound his philosophy. He could no longer attribute these ideas to simply having great personal insight into the troubles of the world. He now knew his anti-consumerism, his understanding of the psychic healing quality of wilderness and some of the very nature of God were revealed to him by God himself. He knew that despite not having all the answers, his writing was divinely inspired.

He began to seek a continuous nexus with the spiritual world. It was something that would consume his life. His sudden interest is starkly reflected in his writing. Prior to January 29th, Winston had a few impersonal comments about God and spirituality, almost as if he were talking about the weather. After his awakening, he becomes frantically compelled to find a direct, intimate connection with God.

When his visions and unusual insight tapered off in February, he described them to a friend who immediately recognized the events as a *Kundalini awakening.*

This psycho-physiological event can be described in the Indian Hindu tradition as a spiritual awakening that grants the subject heightened awareness, contentment, and genius. Kundalini is a Sanskrit word that literally translates to "coiled," as in a coiled snake, and is an "energy" that lies at the base of the spine. The natural state of this energy is dormant, or coiled, and remains unusable unless it is coaxed upward along the spine to the crown of the head, at which time it reaches its full potential to the individual.

In other words, an individual can reach virtual Nirvana, complete happiness and contentment, and release the power of genius, if this energy is tapped. Everyone has Kundalini energy, though most never learn how to raise it and tap into its power.

Kundalini is relatively unfamiliar to the Western world. Indeed Winston had no knowledge of it until after his experience. Many of those in the United States who know of and seek out and practice this Eastern mysticism but have not had extensive experience with the Hindu culture are not likely to understand the subtleties and nuances that resonate within that culture.

This is not "new age," feel-good nonsense practiced by long-haired hippies out of touch with the real world. Spiritual practices around Kundalini have their roots in ancient India and have been in existence longer than Christianity. It predates Islamic and Jewish religions. It was understood thousands of years before the science of psychology. In the sum total of humanity, Kundalini is well accepted.

The psychology surrounding Kundalini was investigated by the pioneering Swiss psychoanalyst Carl Jung, famous for his groundbreaking theories of the subconscious mind. He became fascinated with this Hindu philosophy and attempted to translate this ancient tradition into what was then the new science of psychology.

Jung gave a classic series of lectures on Kundalini in 1932. From these lectures a book was published titled *The Psychology of Kundalini Yoga*. The lectures are essentially a mapping of the ideas and symbolism of Kundalini into modern psychological terms. Jung believed Kundalini described our experiences with the subconscious mind.

Winston used enormous amounts of self-discipline to meditate and discover something within him resulting in the events of January 29th. Perhaps it was a psychological break, or perhaps a Kundalini awakening. Perhaps they are equivalent interpretations of the same event.

Though there are confusing disagreements about the exact methods, the most common way to raise one's Kundalini energy is to practice a specific type of yoga and meditation under the instruction of a guru, or teacher.

"The truth about [Kundalini] spiritual awakening is it optimally leads to ... the discovery of the underlying peace and unity of all things," describes Dr. Bonnie Greenwell. "Many people find inner peace and harmony through these practices."

Dr. Greenwell has assessed more than two thousand practitioners in the Kundalini process over the last twenty-five years. She has authored three books on the subject and is the director of the Kundalini Research Network. She is a recognized expert on the Kundalini process and describes it as a highly positive experience. The vast majority of people who awaken their Kundalini energy are seeking to awaken it.

Winston on the other hand was neither a practitioner nor even much interested in Eastern spiritual philosophy. He felt these types of beliefs were hogwash.

Yet after describing his strange new experiences to Shanna and another friend who understood Kundalini, they concluded this must have been a Kundalini awakening. It was a "very difficult thing to do," she explained. It was an alien idea to him, but as he learned more about Kundalini and its effects, he embraced it as "the only" possible explanation for what was happening to him.

There was just one problem. He never actually attempted to raise his Kundalini energy. For a gift that Kundalini practitioners work to acquire for many months if not years, Winston achieved it by accident. It was certainly not an intentional awakening. This fact did not bother Winston as his experience was only beginning and he did not have a deep understanding of Kundalini. But would his accidental awakening fit with the Eastern understanding of Kundalini?

The fact is he experienced a radical change on January 29th. His friends and family saw it in him. He explicitly wrote of the change. Most importantly, his thoughts inflected from being grounded in daily life to being strange and ephemeral, seeking God and fighting demons.

Some of the other explanations for the sudden change in his thinking and motivation can be ruled out. Winston suffered no head injury, no sickness or disease, no recent drug use, and nothing to indicate a stroke such as a headache or other noticeable neurological deficiency. But the change was surprisingly abrupt, like driving over a cliff. Before January 29th, he wrote about his ascetic philosophy and how to save the planet, mountain biking adventures, and his childhood. Afterward, he is obsessed with the spiritual world, both the beautiful side and the malevolent.

It could have been a Kundalini awakening or it could have been spontaneous and overwhelming mental illness. He was known to push the envelope in all aspects of his life, and his mind was no exception. Winston practiced two methods to push the boundaries of his mind, excessive meditation and psychedelic drugs. Could these have contributed to his change?

Dr. Greenwell opined, "I don't think meditation alone would cause someone to have such a serious break and I would hate to have it appear this way as some groups would use it as a blanket attack against all forms of meditation, which would be a great loss for the many people who have found inner peace and harmony through these practices."

"Generally meditation quiets the mind and teaches someone to settle into the silence within. Most people who warn of the dangers of meditation do not know what they are talking about (from experience) but are afraid of it because it is eastern or because it may distract people from being a good obedient church member. It is true that meditation sometimes brings up unconscious material to be witnessed and released (just as psychotherapy does) and this feels 'dangerous' to some people who find it difficult to look within."

She added, "It can also stir energy and it is helpful to have someone around who understands that this is only your own life force quickening and clearing off old patterns. If Kundalini arises it is helpful to have guidance, but if Winston was borderline and likely to have a break anyway then spiritual guidance might not have been much help. He wouldn't have listened."

One thing would prove to be true, his awakening had fundamentally changed his personality.

Outer Limits

I didn't want a drug that just made me feel good,
I wanted a tool that showed me around the
machinery and explained the workings of things,
so I could learn how to make myself feel good.

W. B. C.

Winston was an explorer of the mind, and along with extensive meditation, he had experimented with hallucinogenic substances, also known as psychedelics. He even describes himself as an "acid head" in his manuscript. That is not to say he was "druggie" or someone who only lives for a good time or escape. Winston used a particular class of mind-altering substances as a means to gain self-awareness, to learn something he did not already know.

The recreational use of psychedelics is a modern phenomenon, infamously popularized, and criminalized, during the 1960s. Before that, the various naturally occurring hallucinogens were used for uncounted centuries, mainly by indigenous people in spiritual or religious ceremonies. The exception of course is lysergic acid diethylamide, or LSD, a relatively modern psychedelic first synthesized in a laboratory in 1938.

It is unfortunate that our society places psychedelics in the same broad category of narcotics that includes cocaine and heroin, because the effects are tremendously different. Psychedelics are not addicting. As a matter of fact they are thought to be useful in breaking addictions to other drugs. They also do not induce the euphoria that is common with narcotics, alcohol and other recreational drugs.

What psychedelics do is alter perception. This effect is not limited to the senses but also internal perception. Thoughts and emotions can be experienced from a different perspective. This is the effect that enhances, or some say deludes, the user's understanding of reality. Some say the use of psychedelics grant insight, others say it is a fantasy. The fact is that humans have ingested these substances from time immemorial in an attempt to gain spiritual connection, knowledge and insight.

Numerous artists, musicians, scientists and other creative and spiritual people have experimented with mind expansion in this manner, and many, if not most, considered these to be profound and positive experiences in their lives.

The late Steve Jobs of Apple thought his experiments with LSD were, "...one of the two or three most important things I have done in my life." Musician Sting said of one particular substance "...[It] has brought me close to something, something fearful and profound and deadly serious." Director Oliver Stone, "...I liked LSD, and I liked peyote.." Author Hunter S. Thompson took it to an extreme, almost constantly experimenting with psychedelics. He felt his experiences helped him break down his inhibitions and bring forth his "strange and terrible" creativity.

The list goes on and crosses the spectrum of every type of genius exhibited by humans. Winston, too, had discovered this gateway into the inner workings of the mind.

He wrote of having taken at times the most commonly available psychedelic substances of mushrooms, acid and mescaline. He had generally positive experiences. His use of these substances did not appear to affect his overall mental health except to possibly improve small aspects of his life for short times. They did not affect his work, his biking or boarding or his ability to intelligently argue a philosophical point.

There was one exception, though. Shanna recalled, "While we were together he was DJ at a party in Oklahoma City and stayed at the house of the promoters. It was then that he tried DMT... It had a tremendous impact on him. He was very fascinated by the entire experience, feeling like you are falling and you cannot stop it, feeling scared and realizing you just need to let go. In this letting go is where he experienced the beauty and peacefulness of the experience."

DMT, or dimethyltryptamine, is quite an interesting substance. It exists naturally in the human body in trace amounts and medical science does not know why. Its chemical structure is similar to psilocybin and psilocin, the psychoactive chemicals in hallucinogenic mushrooms. DMT though, induces interesting subtle differences in the psychedelic experiences of the user.

DMT is extracted from various plants that grow in the jungles of South America. It was first extracted from the roots of *Mimosa Tenuiflora,* a shrub that grows in Brazil. DMT is also found in the leaves of the shrub *Psychotria virdis,* known as *Chacruna* to the native Quechuan people.

It turns out that eating or drinking tea made of the Chacruna leaf has no psychotropic effect. The body metabolizes DMT so quickly that it has no time to affect the brain. But, when Chacruna leaves are cooked in a broth of *Banisteriopsis caapi,* a vine that grows only in the Amazon rain forest, an elixir is produced that has a powerful psychotropic effect.

Banisteriopsis caapi is known to the Quechuan as *Ayahuasca,* The Vine of the Soul. Ayahuasca, pronounced EYE-ah-WOS-ka, contains two substances that act as monoamine oxidase inhibitors, or MOAIs. These substances have no psychedelic effect on the brain by themselves. The effect of the MOAIs, when cooked with DMT laced *Chacruna* leaves is to slow the metabolism of the DMT, which then has time to travel through the bloodstream to the brain.

In other words, drinking a tea made of Chacruna or Ayahuasca alone won't affect you beyond leaving a bad taste in your mouth. Mix the two and you're in for the psychedelic ride of your life.

The psychotropic properties of Ayahuasca tea were well known to primitive tribes inhabiting the ancient jungles of Brazil. For thousands of years this tea has been used for spiritual exploration and healing by these natives, much as peyote and hallucinogenic mushrooms were used by North American natives.

Today, these psychedelic induced spiritual experiences are sold to modern seekers as packaged travel vacations. These "drug tourists" buy all-inclusive trips to primitive villages to undergo Ayahuasca experiences under the supervision of a shaman, or spiritual guide. For many, the visions and insights they experience will change their lives.

The Ayahuasca experience has a dark side. The tea induces relentless nausea and diarrhea. As a matter of fact, the first sign your trip has begun is when you start to vomit. You might then be overwhelmed by terrifying feelings of madness and imminent death. The experiences usually last for hours as your mind is exposed to both ecstatic and horrific feelings and visions that you are unable to control or stop.

DMT seems to be different from other psychedelic drugs. Unlike the more commonly available LSD, peyote or psychedelic mushrooms, DMT users more often report the feelings of a "near death experience." This can be described as a feeling that one is about to die, or actually has died. It includes the feeling of being in the presence of an omnipotent being or beings, moving through a tunnel toward a light, feelings of well being and bliss, and being connected with the universe. There is also the experience of approaching a border to a world from which there is no return, and of a resistance to crossing that border so to return the world of the living.

Near death experiences are not simply drug induced hallucinations but are psychological phenomenon reported by those who have literally approached death, some of whom have actually been pronounced dead but were then resuscitated. This can happen, for example, in a clinical setting when a patient has suffered a potential life-ending event such as cardiac arrest and then revived. The unusual perceptions are so prevalent among those who have been close to death that the phenomena has been categorized and named a Near Death Experience.

Modern medical techniques have given us the ability to revive people who, under the same circumstances in years past, would have died. There are a growing number of people who have been brought back from the brink and so reports of near death experiences have become more common. Despite their increased prevalence there is no scientific explanation for these profound personal journeys.

For unknown reasons DMT tends to mimic these experiences without putting the subject in danger of actually dying. Dr. Rick Strassman, M.D., investigated these phenomena in the early 1990s at the University Of New Mexico School Of Medicine. Sixty volunteers were given hundreds of doses of DMT over a six-year period while Strassman's team studied their subjective experience.

His team found the near death experience described so consistently that he began calling DMT the "God molecule." The results of their study were published in a book called *DMT: The Spirit Molecule*. Strassman explains that unlike LSD, peyote or magic mushrooms, DMT would induce visions of entities. He wrote:

> "When reviewing by bedside
> notes, I continually feel
> surprise in seeing how many of
> our volunteers 'made contact'
> with 'them,' or other beings. At
> least half did so in one form or
> another. Research subjects used
> expressions like 'entities,'
> 'beings,' 'aliens,' 'guides,' and
> 'helpers' to describe them."

His subjects describe these entities as relating to them in some way as if the entities are aware of the subject and are trying to interact with them. Interestingly, the entities are not always good or benign, sometimes they are perceived as being menacing or even evil, almost like angels or demons.

One of Strassman's subjects described a DMT induced near death experience:

> "First I saw a tunnel or
> channel of light off to the
> right. I had to turn to go into
> it. The whole process repeated on
> the left. It was intentional that
> way. It was as if it had a
> source, further away. It got
> bigger and further away, like a
> funnel. It was bright and
> pulsating. There was a sound like
> music, like a score, but it was
> unfamiliar to me, supporting the
> emotional tone of the events and
> drawing me in. I was very small.
> It was very large. There were

large beings in the tunnel, on the right side, next to me. I had a sense of great speed. Everything was unimportant relative to this. Things were flashing, flashing by, as if from a different perspective. It was much more real than life.

The left and right tunnels joined in front of me. There were gremlins, small, faces mostly. They had wings and tails and stuff. I paid them little attention. The larger beings were there to sustain and support me. That was their realm. A sort of good and evil thing: The gremlins versus the tall beings. The tall beings were loving, smiling, serene.

Something rushed through me, out of me. I remember thinking at some point, 'here comes the separation.' I felt my body only when I swallowed or breathed, and that really wasn't a physical feeling as much as a way of setting ripples through the experience. I felt strongly, 'this is dying and this is okay.' "

Just as many of the subjects of Strassman's study, Winston also described his DMT trip as having the characteristics of a near death experience, the feelings of uncontrollable falling, the bliss that comes from letting go. Because this had such a great impact on him, this raises the question as to whether he subsequently sought out the near death experience in other ways by physically pushing his body near death to recapture that experience.

Whatever his motivations, Winston had a proclivity to experiment with the wild, beautiful, terrible and dangerous territories of his mind.

Winston had not ingested psychedelics or any other drug in the months leading up to his awakening. There was no direct link between his awakening experience and any mind-altering substance. He was, however, practicing another exercise to push his mental experience and that was extreme meditation.

The term "meditation" has many interpretations, but a general description might be that it is the mental exercise to change one's wakeful state of awareness or consciousness. Excluding the unconscious, or coma state, there are three classes of consciousness: Sleep, dreaming and wakefulness. Though it may seem that sleep and dreaming are the same state, they are quite different in terms of how the brain behaves and the psychological reactions to each. These states can be measured by brainwaves, rapid eye movement, and other biological changes.

Meditation is an exercise to alter the wakeful state, and those who practice meditation have little doubt that it does alter consciousness. There are many scientific studies that show brainwave and biological changes that happen during meditation, implying that there is indeed an alteration of consciousness.

There are numerous meditation techniques, some relatively new and some dating back to time immemorial. They all have the same goal, to calm and focus the ever-active mind. This is usually accomplished by sitting in a quiet room and focusing on a single thought such as your breath or a spot behind your forehead. All other distracting thoughts must be quieted. This is quite difficult to do at first, thoughts seem to come from nowhere and grab your attention. But like any form of learning, practice makes perfect. You can achieve a quiet state more quickly and hold it longer in time.

The effects of meditation are usually positive. It relaxes and centers the individual. It helps with concentration. Many feel it helps improve minor psychological difficulties such as anxiety and restlessness. However, psychologists have accumulated a growing body of evidence that suggests sometimes meditation can be harmful. In rare instances meditation has been linked to the development of serious psychological problems.

These include relaxation-induced anxiety, which is a paradoxical anxious feeling that becomes more intense as the patient relaxes. Also reported are epileptic episodes and involuntary movements such as facial tics and the head suddenly twisting forty-five degrees. The most common problems are dissociation, which is the loss of association of thoughts that are normally associated, such as unexplained "spacey" feelings, hearing voices of people who are not there, and depersonalization, which is the loss of reality of one's self or environment.

Patients who suffered these symptoms had been practicing one of the many types of meditation such as Transcendental Meditation as popularized by the Maharishi Mahesh Yogi (the spiritual advisor to the Beatles). This practice teaches concentration on a personalized mantra, or saying, or a yogic meditation that emphasizes concentrating on breathing, etc. What the patients all had in common was the excessive amount of time spent in meditation, sometimes hours every day for months or even years.

Prominent psychologist Dr. Margaret Singer (deceased) who was a clinical psychologist emeritus at the University of California at Berkeley, and research partner Dr. Janja Lalich did a prominent case study of seventy patients who reported psychological problems from excessive meditation.

Among their findings was a thirty-six year old business executive who cannot work and lives off welfare as a result of the relentless anxiety attacks and blackouts he suffered after taking up meditation. "Everything gets in through my senses," he told Singer.

Another example was a young woman who suffered hallucinations of seeing rooms fill with orange fog when she "spaced out" at random moments. And after practicing excessive meditation, a twenty-six year old man became overwhelmed by rage and sexual urges whenever he went out in public, driving him to stay home to avoid these episodes.

None of the subjects in their study had any prior mental illness, nor did they have a family history of mental illness.

Problems arising from meditation such as these are rare. However, Winston himself had shown a rare ability to focus on a task to an extreme. "Winston meditated for hours every day after he returned from Silverton," Shanna explained. Jonathan noted this as well. "Winston would meditate through his ideas more than ever," he said.

Winston summarized his goal in these meditations:

I can't seem to push through that extra step into that non-physical world, a place I visit daily in my 3 hour meditations, a place I refer to now as home...

It was apparent that Winston was seeking some sort of out-of-this-world experience that he may have touched during his meditative experiences. He seemed to have achieved his goal with his awakening, at least partially. After January 29th, he began experiencing spontaneous dissociative events, what he described as trances or "coma experiences."

Throughout the month of February, he experienced an intense series of these trances that he wrote of in his manuscript. Through these trances he solidified his belief in a metaphysical world where "Gods" and demons were as real as day and night:

> *..so in part I thought that I would eventually succeed in my "meditating myself to death" and that the experiences I was having now within these trances were perhaps the result of someone finding me immediately after a successful attempt.*
>
> *...when I was experiencing the "coma," and my friends would come in but and I would react to who they were without me (my physical self) knowing who they were, except these "people" or "Gods" that I was meeting, and there had to have been between 6 and 12 of these "Gods" because I often had the sense of at least two Gods in the "room" with me...*

In early February, a few days after his Kundalini experience, Winston begins fasting. He intends to fast for forty days "... as Jesus did in the desert."

During his fast, he has no contact with the outside world. Though he leaves his condo to exercise or walk Townshend, he speaks to none of his friends and has no phone or internet connection. He continues to write and exercise excessively.

By early March his five foot, eleven inch frame has dropped from one hundred fifty pounds to one hundred thirty-five. He becomes distraught at his failures to find a spiritual connection. He decides one morning to kill himself by taking fifty phenobarbital pills, a medication left over from when Townshend was being treated for seizures. He loses consciousness.

But he does not die. Winston regains consciousness several days later. He calls 9-1-1 and an ambulance arrives to rescue him. A day later he is placed in the psychiatric ward at University Hospital in Aurora, Colorado.

From the time Winston began his fast in February though the first week of March, he would have been constantly reminded of his hunger. It would have been increasingly difficult to do anything athletic or to concentrate on his writing. In fact his writing did decrease significantly over this period. All the while he would have been reminded that he was starving in the land of plenty, pitting his willpower against his primal desire to eat while constantly tempted by savory food easily available to him.

It is one thing to walk into a desert to fast, away from all people and temptation. Winston did it in metropolitan area, surrounded by the temptations of restaurants, grocery stores, food ads, and the mouthwatering aroma of his neighbor's barbeque.

Psychiatric Hospital

"The psychological symptoms [of Kundalini syndrome] tend to mimic schizophrenia. It is very likely, therefore, that such individuals may be diagnosed as schizophrenics and be either institutionalized or given very drastic and unwarranted treatment...I dare to guess, on the basis of discussions with my psychiatrist-friends, that this process is not as exotic and rare as one would like to believe, and possibly 25 to 30 percent of all institutionalized schizophrenics belong to this category..."

Itzhak Bentov, *Stalking the Wild Pendulum: The Mechanics of Consciousness*
1988

March, 2008. University Hospital Psychiatric Ward, Aurora, Colorado. Winston tried to kill himself. The psychiatrists treating him assumed there *must* have been something wrong in his mind. He was prescribed Risperidone, an antipsychotic used in the treatment of schizophrenia. However, his doctors could not make a definitive diagnosis of anything actually wrong with Winston. His behavior was well within the norm. He was highly, even annoyingly, functional.

His body recovered rapidly as he ate regular meals. He was soon up and about, interacting with the other mental patients in the hospital. One afternoon in the TV room he noticed other patients enjoying a NASCAR race. Winston felt frustration. He did not see a popular sports show. He saw irony and hypocrisy.

> *...I mean here we are in the middle of a "war", where people are fighting and dying in Iraq to essentially secure oil fields for big business that run society and driving cars in circles as if gasoline were something that was oozing freely from the ground, which it may be, but it isn't oozing freely into our tanks or hands, its being middleman'd and sold back to us by a not so covert big business elite, but the bottom line being that our sons and brothers and daughters are dying in order to secure it for that not so covert elite, we aren't securing it directly for the people...*

Despite existing in a safe, calming environment and under medication, Winston the Philosopher continued to focus on his philosophy and the problems with society.

On a more personal level, he was deeply affected by his observations of treatment received by his fellow patients in the ward. He was empathetic to their lack of human contact:

> *I can sense a lack of compassion in here, but apparently it's illegal for them to use it; no hugs, no holding of the hand, no sitting on the bed while you cry, it's all been made illegal by our own bureaucracy. There seems to be enough nurses and doctors in here to take everyone aside for a minute or two a day and maybe hold their hands while they cry or walk with them for a lap or two around the halls, but they seem stuck on the wrong side of the counter; glued to computer screens, filling out paper work, or researching which designer anti-psychotic will suit their customer the best.*

Winston tried to help in what little ways he could. He talked and joked with the other patients in an attempt to give them some sort of human comfort. Of one experience he wrote:

> *"Debbie" was a 52 year old Mother of two, who as far as I can see simply broke down one day, but she's still in there, you can see her every now and then, but for the most part she's so drugged up (probably as a form of protection to her consciousness) but when she does speak she essentially repeats herself, and jumps around in subject matter to things that aren't pertinent to whatever it was you might have been briefly talking about, but occasionally you'd get this glimpse of her, and you'd try to hold onto it, but it wouldn't last very long; she did best when you asked her to listen to something you were about to*

tell her, but I wasn't able to actually do that until the final day I was there, but to me the breakthrough we had, however brief was extremely powerful, and while I was telling her what I was trying to tell her I could see that she was there, absorbing it, and straining to take as much as she could in, and that was the most I "saw" of her the entire time I was there, and I'll explain that situation a little clearer here.

Debbie had been there since the day I had been admitted, and she seemed to get progressively worse during my/her stay there, at first she wasn't 'heavily' medicated, but she would ramble and just constantly talk and say things that had truth, but connect them to things that weren't real. She would tell you daily that her Son, or Husband was coming to pick her up that day, and that she would be leaving, the first couple times she actually would convince me that this was actually happening by adding her own details that offered some sense of validity to the picture, but eventually I realized that she was just making it all up, but she was clear and rational about it (to some degree) but she progressively worsened as she was there, exploding and breaking down emotionally over things that were essentially trivial, and sometimes nonexistent.

By my final day there they had her so heavily medicated that she couldn't really walk or talk all that well, she was less coherent than she'd been since I'd met her, but I wanted to tell her goodbye and I wanted to give her some parting advice or comfort before I left, so at dinner I sat down with her, after I cut up some of her meat for her, and read her a couple of the cards she had gotten, I crouched down next to her, so she didn't have to look up at me, from where I was she could just turn her head and her eyes would meet mine with no effort on her part.

"Debbie" I said. "I have something I want to tell you so I want you to really listen to me, and I want to see that you're listening before I tell you what I want to tell you." "I'm leaving today and I want to tell you something, do you understand me?" "I'm leaving too", she said. "No", I said, "I want you to just listen to me, because I want to tell you something, but I want to make sure you're listening, ok?" "Ok", she said. "I think you're going through a little storm right now, and I think that you just have to hold on until you get through it and you see some blue sky." "You need to keep that in your heart and remember that." "Just hang on and in time you'll come through the other end, because you're a fighter, aren't you?" "I'm a fighter", she said. "You just got to weather this storm, and keep looking for that blue sky, and know that God will help you come through it ok, it just might take a little while, do you understand?" "Yes", she says, "I'm a fighter."

I repeated this a few times to her in slightly different variations and I have to believe that I could feel like she was there listening, and hoping that she would at least hold on to some of it and tap into during the night, or whatever bad episodes she might be going through, as if it were a verbal lighthouse sitting there out in the distance peaking through that fog, a piece of hope. I felt like I had to leave her with something, and I didn't know what else I could offer to her that would be any use, and a simple goodbye didn't offer me any console.

    I might never know if it did any good for her, but it sure made me feel as if I was trying to do something, and I think I realize now that, this is what I need from the world that I'm not getting; that sense that you're having an effect on it, and on people, but I know in my heart that what I really need is that feeling on a massive scale in order to "get better" myself, and I'm not so sure sometimes that I might ever see that, but I need to try.

Winston wasn't trying to cure anyone, he was making a sincere attempt to communicate with, and comfort, another human being. Through that he discovered something about himself. He needed to have an effect on the world.

The psychiatrists saw something different. They felt Winston was interfering with their prescribed treatment of Debbie. "The doctors were not happy with Winston doing this," Jovanka laughed as she related the story of the sane, compassionate man amongst the crazy.

Winston was discharged from the hospital approximately one week after being admitted. Jovanka made the two-hour drive to Aurora to pick up her brother. She drove him back to her house in Colorado Springs, offering him a place to stay, something that would be a stable environment where she hoped Winston would begin his re-entry into a normal, healthy life.

His suicide attempt was shocking to Jovanka. "I never would have thought he would do that," she said as she recalled the incident of starvation in his Lakewood condo. "When I picked him up at the hospital he looked terrible." She was equally surprised at his new interest in religion.

The Mersmans live in a quiet, expansive neighborhood just at the point between the eastern plains and the base of Pikes

Peak. Their comfortable house takes in a panoramic view of the Front Range Mountains and is within walking distance of the edge of town where the suburbs give way to the rustic forested foothills. It is an ideal setting for a relaxed convalescence.

Jovanka's lifestyle was almost diametrically opposite to that of her brother. She and her husband Dennis were raising their two adolescent children in middle class comfort and stability. Jovanka has a pleasant but serious demeanor, is self-confident and cheerful. She is not timid about expressing her opinions.

Dennis is a self-assured man of few words, but they are always thoughtful. Both Jovanka and Dennis work full time in professional fields and are the epitome of stability. They enjoy the comforts afforded to them and like the vast majority of America, have no qualms about material possessions or wealth. They work hard to provide for their children and themselves, are well entrenched in the American way of life and see nothing inherently wrong with it.

There was an obvious clash of ideals and philosophy between Winston and Jovanka, but it was never acrimonious or spiteful. Jovanka would get frustrated and angry at times at Winston's actions, but Winston would act the role of a wise sage, trying to teach Jovanka and Dennis to see the light, so to speak.

Jovanka and Dennis never really understood why Winston pursued some of the ideas he did, but they were fascinated by them and made an honest effort to understand. Winston had earned their respect through his intelligence and the passion he felt about his life and philosophy. But it must have been like trying to understand a wise old Chinese sage who could not speak a word of English. Much was lost in translation.

Jovanka offered her brother a room in her basement where he began to re-enter life. The Mersmans soon discovered that Winston's ascetic, anti-consumerist philosophy was not the only thing different thing about him. "He would always cook up rice and beans and not eat the meals we prepared," Jovanka recalled, and he would "hike in the foothills for twelve hours at a time."

And he pushed on with his manuscript. He became reflective of the events since his Kundalini awakening, writing:

> *3.22.2008*
> *I've been flipping back in order to edit some of the things that I had written during the fasting period, I can't even clearly remember when I gave up food altogether, there doesn't seem to be a definitive and clear date, but it doesn't really matter at this point, it had to be around the first of February. As I read some of things I have written I wonder if I should edit it at all, because the clarity I have now is not exactly what was going on then. I know that at times I was drifting through periods of insanity, and it somewhat comes through in the scribble that I laid down, so perhaps I should let the reader fend for themselves, I'll decide what to do later, but will at least reflect now as it is still fresh in my mind.*

Schizophrenia is characterized by disorganized thinking and loss of emotional responsiveness. The name literally translates as "split mind," or a mind that has been broken. Though the disease exhibits certain definite symptoms, it cannot be detected through biological or physical means. There is no medical test that indicates you have or are likely to suffer schizophrenia. The only way it can be diagnosed is through direct interview via self-reported symptoms, and direct study of the patient by a psychiatrist. And it is often misdiagnosed as bipolar disorder or borderline personality disorder, among others. It is not a simple disease.

Symptoms of schizophrenia include delusions, auditory and visual hallucinations, paranoia, disorganized thinking, and emotional and social withdrawal. Some with a profound case become catatonic, unresponsive to external stimuli.

Winston was certainly suffering from a mental disturbance, but was it schizophrenia or something else? What is of extreme interest to note is that while it is true he was given antipsychotic drugs used in the treatment of schizophrenia, his actual condition was somewhat of a mystery to his doctors.

He exhibited some of the symptoms of schizophrenia such as hallucinations, visions and bizarre delusions. But his thinking was not disorganized, a hallmark symptom of the disease. He was discharged from the hospital with no diagnosed mental disease and was not prescribed any further antipsychotic medications or scheduled follow-up visits.

Is it possible he was experiencing the negative effects of an Kundalini awakening, a condition known as Kundalini *syndrome*? This condition mimics schizophrenia but exhibits important differences, differences that more closely matched Winston's condition.

Kundalini expert Dr. Bonnie Greenwell explained, "When a person with activated [Kundalini] energy does not eat or get enough sleep it is easy for delusional experiences to arise. The lines between relative reality and dream become very thin. Anyone who doesn't sleep for a while can show signs of psychosis, and there is no question this can be amplified if Kundalini is active. Many people with active Kundalini will experience an occasional vision and will begin to see the world in a different way than the status quo, but these are usually positive experiences and not troublesome in the way psychotic images and fantasies are. But if there is not enough sleep and confused understanding there can be a spinning out of control that can lead to hospitalization. It is not uncommon for such people to be deemed okay once they are rested and to be released from a hospital at that point. This may have been the case with [Winston]... Certainly if he was open to guidance from someone experienced in the process it would have helped him, but it is possible he had an underlying disturbance that would have made him resist good advice."

Hindu philosophical thought interprets these schizophrenia-like symptoms as an incorrect Kundalini awakening. Instead of experiencing the spiritual ecstasy and awareness during a proper rising of the Kundalini energy, those experiencing Kundalini syndrome will suffer the symptoms very similar to what Winston unwittingly described. He felt the energy, but in a chaotic form he did not understand.

He experienced significant negative symptoms not normally associated with a Kundalini awakening, including his visual hallucinations, pain and feeling of illness. For practitioners of Kundalini, this might have been recognized as a serious problem that should be rectified in haste.

In his 1932 lectures transcribed in *The Psychology of Kundalini Yoga,* Carl Jung recognized how an unmanaged Kundalini awakening can give rise to a schizophrenic state:

> "...It is as if the Kundalini in its movement upward were pulling us up with it, as if we were part of that movement.
>
> When the upheaval comes, we are carried with it and naturally we might think we are moving upward. But it makes, of course, a tremendous difference whether one flies, or whether it is a wave or a great wind that lifts one. For to fly is one's own activity, and one can safely come down again, but when one is carried upward, it is not under one's control, and one will be put down after a while in a most

disagreeable way - then it means
a catastrophe. So, you see, it is
wise not to identify with these
experiences ... Otherwise you get
an inflation, and inflation is
just a minor form of lunacy...
And if you get absolutely
inflated that you burst, it is
schizophrenia."

The process Jung described in an academic lecture in Bern, Switzerland, was to be experienced in real life a few years later, thousands of miles away, by an Indian man who, after falling into the void of Kundalini syndrome, would suffer an epic struggle to regain sanity and ultimately, bliss.

Pandit Gopi Krishna, the Indian yogi who later was to become perhaps the greatest influence in popularizing Kundalini in the Western world, experienced a spontaneous awakening that drove him to the brink of psychosis.

Born in 1903 in the Himalayan Provence of Kashmir, Gopi Krishna entered a life of hardship. His father abandoned the family, leaving his mother to raise him along with his two young sisters. As the eldest male in the family, high expectations were placed on the young Krishna.

He grew to become a natural athlete who was fond of the sport of wrestling. Though studious, he failed to pass college entrance exams and subsequently became a common laborer. Unfulfilled, he began to meditate in an attempt to discover himself.

Krishna meditated "unsupervised," as he explained, every morning for many years. At the age of 34, he experienced a sudden rush of energy he described as "a roar like that of a waterfall, I felt a stream of light enter my brain through my spinal cord." Instead of being a positive experience, though, it triggered mild psychosis and it soon felt as if he would die. He experienced sleep depravation, visions, and a nearly complete loss of appetite over the next two months.

Krishna reasoned that his Kundalini had risen incorrectly and began a series of exercises to correct his state. He was ultimately successful after enduring twenty-five years of effort to find the correct balance of diet, exercise and mental discipline.

In the end, Gopi Krishna obtained a stable Kundalini awakening in which he experienced all the positive effects, a state that he described as "superconsciousness" in his autobiographical book *Kundalini: The Evolutionary Energy in Man,* first published in 1967.

Much of Hindu philosophy, including Kundalini, is understood in different terms in Western thought. Modern psychology recognizes the rare, but real, disorders that can be produced by mental and spiritual practices.

The *Diagnostic and Statistical Manual of Mental Disorders,* or DSM, is the overarching guide for diagnosis used by medical psychiatric treatment professionals in the United States. The fourth version, DSM-IV, published in 1994, recognized these problems as a distinguishable condition. Though not specifically mentioned, Kundalini syndrome falls under the "Religious or Spiritual Problem" diagnosis.

The DSM-IV cautions that this condition should not be treated as a mental disorder.

Visions

My wife knew nothing of the life and death struggle in which I was engaged, but alarmed by my strange behavior, lack of appetite, bodily disturbances, constant walks, and above all by the never-lifting cloud of anxiety and gloom on my face, she advised me again and again to consult a physician...

...My brother-in-law could not grasp the significance of what I related to him, but said that his guru had once remarked that if by mistake Kundalini were aroused [incorrectly] there was every danger of serious psychic and physical disturbances, ending in permanent disability, insanity, or death.

Gopi Krishna, *Kundalini, the Evolutionary Energy in Man*
1967

Shanna recalled that Winston's personality was "different" after his release from the hospital. Though generally lucid, she thought his ideas had become strange. It may have been the result of his second transformational experience of approaching death through fasting two months prior (the first transformational experience being Winston's spontaneous Kundalini awakening).

"One day he called me and said he ran into a famous author while hiking on Green Mountain. He said it was Zechria Stichin, author of the book *12th Planet.* He wanted me to go with him to visit this author at his place in Golden. We drove over to this house and Winston knocked on the door. The people inside had no idea who he was talking about. He returned to the car very confused, he was sure he had the right address."

She paused and added, "Maybe this was some sort of psychological break."

Later, in a small coffee shop in Denver, Winston began explaining the importance of certain numbers. He was emphatic about what he saw as patterns in the symbols and signs around him, like hidden messages that told him things.

She said, "there was nothing there, I couldn't figure out what he was talking about. It really reminded me of that guy in the movie *A Beautiful Mind* who saw all those messages that weren't really there."

Mathematician and Nobel Prize laureate John Nash, the subject of the book and movie *A Beautiful Mind,* is portrayed as having seen hidden messages in newspaper and magazine articles and advertisements. These messages were communications to him from a mysterious organization. It turns out that these messages did not exist, they were the hallucinations of his schizophrenic mind.

Winston's interest in numbers and symbols was nothing new. He had always been intrigued with mathematical curiosities, to the point of naming his cafe after the Mobius loop, a simple one-sided object that has no beginning and no end.

Anyone can construct a Mobius loop. Imagine you want to make a paper bracelet. You cut a strip of paper and attach the ends together. At that point you have a simple loop. If, however, you put a half-twist in one end and attach the ends, you now have a Mobius loop. Without lifting your finger, you can touch the loop at one point and run completely around twice to end where you began. It has only one side. It has no beginning and no end.

This was an important symbol to Winston. What appears to be a two-sided object is actually one, and because it is a loop, there is no beginning and no end. The religious and philosophical symbolism is obvious. He wanted the Mobius Cafe to be a place that brought people together, perhaps to ask whether we really *are* all one, and one with the universe, even if we appear separate.

Winston's fascination was in both the mathematics and the metaphor. His intrigue with such curiosities was amplified after his release from the hospital. His mind began to see importance in numbers and symbols more than anyone else did.

He wrote incessantly about the significance of why certain numbers, symbols and colors appeared as they did in our perception of them. He related the shape of number symbols to the significance of their ordinal value. In other words, he said there is a reason that the number six follows the number five and it is related to the visual impression of the symbols "6" and "5".

One chapter of Winston's manuscript titled *Numbers* is about an intriguing, though rambling, explanation of the meaning of the base ten digits:

> *The number 0 represents a cell or the planet earth or God...*

The number 1 would be assumed to be something that stands below all creation...

The number 2 would be the form of a perfect human...

The number 3 would be modern, or 'incomplete' man..

The number 4 is an interesting little bugger because it has the qualities of both numbers and letters... '4' represents language...

The number 5 is characteristic of a profile of an open mouth with a nose above it... It is commanding, but not specific to vocal commands... It depends on the '4' used...

The number 6 represents that which contains and nourishes life... It represents a sprouting seed...

The number 7 represents a tool or a key... and symbolizes all male life forms on the planet...

The number 8 represents the beginnings of the first life on earth... It has the physical characteristics of first division of a cell... It is the keyhole of which the key unlocks, the other half of 7 [female]...

The number 9 represents the result of 7 and 8 and resembles a profile view of an early life form in embryonic stage...

Many in cultures around the world attach significance to this type of symbolic numerology, but lately Winston was taking it a step further and beginning to see messages that no one else saw.

At that meeting in the coffee shop with Shanna, Winston also proudly displayed his latest adornment. He had permanently tattooed red dots the size of thumbtacks on the inside of each wrist and at the top of his nose exactly between his eyes.

"He said it helped with reception," Shanna related. I asked her if Winston's forehead tattoo was a *Talik,* the red dot worn on the forehead throughout the Indian subcontinent representing the "mind's eye," a symbol of Hindu religious devotion. "I have no idea what it meant," she said, "but I know it wasn't related to any Hindu practice, or any other religion. He came up with it on his own."

Winston's manuscript revealed his growing interest with the red dots, especially between the eyes, beginning about one month after being released from the hospital. Initially he paints the dot on every morning, but is soon compelled to make it permanent. He finds a tattoo parlor in Colorado Springs to do the job and proudly emerges with the markings for the world to see. He writes that they will be used for "his own spiritual benefit."

In his manuscript, Winston also specifically denies this was a Talik. In an imaginary conversation between God and himself, Winston writes that this is "not what the Hindus wear. It is different."

The Talik is worn all over India for slightly varying reasons, ranging from fashion to religious devotion to a particular Hindu god. All of these purposes have one root. The dot represents the "third eye," or mind's eye, and a spiritual connection.

In tantric yoga, the Talik has a particular use. It helps retain the Kundalini energy in the body. There is no evidence that Winston had any knowledge of this ancient practice whatsoever, but it is an interesting coincidence.

The last thing that Winston and Shanna spoke about at the coffee shop was Winston's plans for a forty-five day solo trek through the mountains along the Colorado Trail. Shanna broke down and began to cry.

"I had just seen that movie *Into the Wild* and I could see this happening to Winston."

The movie *Into the Wild* is a fictionalized account of the last journey and demise of Christopher McCandless, who famously died of starvation in the Alaskan wilderness.

Revelation

*"Both revelation and delusion are attempts at the solution of problems.
Artists and Scientists realize that no solution is ever final, but that each
new creative step points the way to the next artistic or scientific
problem. In contrast, those who embrace religious revelations and
delusional systems tend to see them as unshakeable and permanent.
Religious faith is an answer to the problem of life... The majority of
mankind want or need some all-embracing belief system which
purports to provide an answer to life's mysteries, and are not
necessarily dismayed by the discovery that their belief system, which
they proclaim as "The Truth", is incompatible with the beliefs of other
people. One man's faith is another man's delusion... whether a belief is
considered to be a delusion or not depends partly upon the intensity
with which it is defended, and partly upon the numbers of people
subscribing to it."* [1]
*First they call you a crazy heretic, then they address you as Jesus
Christ, Lord and Savior. Ohh, the irony.*

W. B. C.

---

[1] This quoted text appears in Winston's manuscript and is from *Feet of
Clay: Saints, Sinners, and Madmen* by Anthony Storr. This quote also
appears in *Under the Banner of Heaven: A Story of Violent Faith* by Jon
Krakauer, which was Winston's source. Ironically, Winston wrote of his
fascination with *Under the Banner of Heaven* but had never read the
story his life was most compared to, that of Christopher McCandless
portrayed in Krakauer's *Into the Wild*.

Mid-July, 2008. Collegiate Peaks, Colorado. From a campsite somewhere near Mount Yale, under a clear night sky brightly illuminated by the full moon, Winston penned an entry in his Colorado Trail journal. He wrote of recent events, like the cute blonde hiker he met earlier that day. He wrote of life on the trail, Townshend losing one bootie, and his last pen running out of ink.

He wrote of the rain and the pesky mosquitos. He wrote of the pleasurable experience of eating. And he wrote of God. Winston was searching for signs and direction as to how he should complete his mission of leading the planet to a culture of sharing, responsible use and appreciation of the beauty of nature rather than that of greed and destruction.

Winston admits he will go as far as dying if it is the will of God. After all, he is wandering the wilderness on the Colorado Trail at the behest of God Himself. Winston felt his sole purpose in life was to find and follow that next request from God.

That was the latest step in his spiritual journey that began with his Kundalini awakening, through his fasting and suicide attempt, recovery in the hospital and at Jovanka's house. After his release from the psychiatric hospital, Winston decided he needed to find out what the world had already learned about God. He began to study the precepts, morals, writings and beliefs of as many religions as he could.

These studies were driven by two burning questions on his mind: "Why am I alive?" and "What is my purpose?" After having survived such tremendous suffering and a near-death experience, he was perplexed as to why he did not die, and became even further entrenched in the belief that there must be a higher purpose for him, a purpose ordained by God.

Because he was now more open than ever to the questions of religion, spirituality and God, Jovanka suggested to her brother that he read the Bible. The Mersmans were church-going Catholics and invited Winston to come along to mass. Winston couldn't help but note that the weekend immediately following his release was Easter. He went along and was impressed by the sermon and the dedication of the priest.

During his recovery days at the Mersmans home Winston read the Bible cover to cover between long hikes and hours of meditation. He was back to his regular pre-hospitalization routine of exercise and meditation but more bent on understanding God from the point of view of established religions.

The last week of May, Winston decided to travel down to Alamosa, Colorado, to visit his mother. Alamosa is located on a high plain in the south-central Colorado highlands. The plain is astoundingly flat, like the still surface of a great lake. In the distance rise the dramatically steep Sangre de Cristo Mountains to the east, and the San Juan Mountains to the west. It is a modest size town with a population of more than eight thousand, yet it has a strange atmosphere surrounding it.

Much of that strangeness comes from its location in the middle of the San Luis valley. The Sangre de Cristo Mountains, literally "Blood of Christ," so named by the Spanish due to the unusual red color of some of the sharp, bizarre shaped high peaks. The Great Sand Dunes heaping over 700 feet, the largest in North America, lie at the foot of the Sangres. The valley is a desert, yet abundant water gurgles up from numerous natural springs.

Spanish legends of hidden gold and ghosts permeate the valley's history. In modern times, the San Luis valley has become famous for UFO sightings. No one knows why, but perhaps the deep darkness at night and the clarity of the high altitude air, and the isolation from the rest of civilization, somehow reveal phenomena unnoticed elsewhere.

It was in this setting that Winston delved more deeply into his own spiritual and religious exploration. He continued his religious studies, his hours-long meditations and his day long hikes. From the local library, he checked out and read the entire Bhagavad Gita, one of the ancient Hindu scriptures. When he was done, he exchanged that book for another about the Dead Sea Scrolls. He finished that and read another about the Wakan Tanka, the Sioux Indian sacred way of life.

This was his way of dealing with his obsession to answer the ongoing questions in his mind. Even though he was ostensibly visiting his mother for an emotional connection, reassurance and to attempt to ground himself in the real world, Winston was probably well beyond any help that his mother could give. He had lived his adult life with minimal contact with her and so they both felt somewhat out of touch and at a loss for understanding each other. Winston's writings at this time describe very little real connection with Mirjana.

In the end, though his sister and mother both helped sustain him, providing for basic needs such as food and a place to stay, they ultimately could not reach him emotionally or intellectually. Winston was his own man and was determined to follow his own path.

During his final days in Alamosa, Winston increased the hours he spent meditating, concentrating on his breathing until he experienced another breakthrough. On June 8th, 2008 he wrote:

> *There were two bright flashes last night that woke me up in my room, amazing, silent, white flashes, one right after the other, and I had the sensation I was weightless and falling for a second, wonderfully strange.*

He didn't know it at the time but he was on the brink of yet another upheaval in his life. The next day he boarded a Greyhound bus bound for Colorado Springs. He penned an entry into his manuscript:

I keep having visions of me doing the Colorado Trail on this bus ride, as if I'm supposed to prepare everything as soon as I get back, so that I can be on the trail by Summer's Solstice. And I complain to God why these thoughts and feelings are coming up while I look out at the country side to my left, and we cruise by it, because I see how impractical the plan would be to undertake such an endeavor, not because I physically couldn't do it, but because I don't have the necessary gear, food, money etc... I would be asking people, like my sister, Jonathan, Shawn, and Shanna, who all work at least forty hours a week to provide for themselves, and/or their families, I would be asking these people to basically finance this "spiritual journey" of mine, so that I could take the entire summer, and my entire life for that matter, off, from my already grueling schedule, so that I could go hike 500 miles of trail through the Mountains of Colorado. Do you see where I might have a problem with asking for that?

Pilgrimage

The wilderness once offered men a
plausible way of life, now it
functions as a psychiatric
refuge. Soon there will be no
wilderness. Soon there will be no
place to go. Then the madness
becomes universal and the
universe goes mad.

Edward Abbey, *The Monkey Wrench Gang*
1975

Jovanka picked up her brother at the bus station in downtown Colorado Springs. During the twenty-minute drive back to her house, Winston broke the news that he had decided to hike the Colorado Trail. Jovanka could not hide her frustration and anger. She viewed this decision as frivolous and irresponsible.

She pointed out to her brother that she was helping to get him back on his feet and had no intention to provide room and board indefinitely. He needed to take charge of his life, to find his own place. To Winston, however, this conversation was simply confirming that he would not be returning to the Mersmans house after his Colorado Trail trek. This did not bother him because he did not feel he would need to return. Jovanka's practical attitude did not sway his decision whatsoever; he felt he must hit the trail within the next couple of weeks. By the summer solstice.

Jovanka then tells Winston that he has a tax return check waiting at her place. He had failed to file his tax return for 2005, though he had filled out the form. Jovanka had found Winston's return in the papers she picked up from his Lakewood condo. At first Winston had little reaction, he thought it might be a few hundred dollars at most. When he got back to the Mersmans house he didn't even open the envelope right away. He was more concerned about how he would cover the cost of his hiking supplies. He thought of his good friend Jonathan Wrobel, someone who could set him up with equipment from REI.

When Winston opened the envelope he was taken aback. The check from the IRS was worth $3700. It was more than enough to cover his expenses. To Winston, this was not a mere coincidence or a nice surprise (due to Jovanka's diligence), it was an inscrutable sign from God. After all, he had been obsessed with hiking the Colorado Trail and getting started before the solstice, only eleven days away. To him this solved all his problems and opened all the doors.

He could have used his unexpected windfall in a practical way, as seed money to start his life anew. He could have gotten a job at a bike shop or a cafe, rented a place of his own and re-started his life. Instead he chose a pilgrimage in the wilderness. His choice was not surprising when viewed in the light of two truths Winston well understood about himself; He would not be happy in a conventional nine-to-five life, and he was experiencing a spiritual revolution.

Even if he had not received what he perceived as his revelation from God, Winston felt he was not fit to begin a conventional life, at least not at this time. A couple of months in the backcountry among the trees and fresh mountain air while contemplating his ideas and philosophies may be just what the doctor ordered, he thought. He would renew and rejuvenate in his beloved wilderness. And just maybe that was what God intended for him.

The Colorado Trail is a walking route that begins in the foothills just outside of Denver and winds five hundred miles southwest across the state, ending in Durango. It traverses along the base of 14,000 foot high mountains, over passes above timberline, through meadows and forests of pine and aspen, occasionally crossing a road but otherwise entirely in the backcountry. Though not as popular or as long as the Appalachian Trail, the Colorado Trail sees its share of through-hikers.

An end-to-end trekker can cover the entire route in approximately forty-five days. Most of the trail is far from any town, requiring through-hikers to carry a full complement of lightweight camping gear including a tent, sleeping bag, camp stove, fuel and food.

Supplies can be replenished along the way as the trail passes near small towns such as Baily, Breckenridge, Buena Vista, and Creede. Winston's plan was to replenish supplies as necessary, and to ask Jovanka and Jonathan to support him by mailing care packages of essentials that may be unavailable in the small mountain towns.

Though he chose to do the trek alone, he did take Townshend as his companion. Jovanka drove the two of them to the starting point outside of Denver on June 20 and they departed the trailhead. Winston and Townshend hiked twenty miles and set up their camp before the summer solstice arrived at 5:59 p.m. that evening.

Winston made only terse entries in his journal for the first five days. He wrote of the weather, equipment issues, minor difficulties of trekking, Townshend's behavior, elk that he saw and other minutia of wilderness trekking.

On June 24, he writes of the rain, details of the meals he prepares, his equipment, Band-Aids for blisters, and snow patches around his campsite. He feels better; his psyche is healing now. He mentions drinking freshly melted snow and likens it to "holy water." He has strange dreams, vividly hears drums and birds in his tent while asleep. Terse references to God.

Winston and Townshend somewhere along the Colorado Trail.

Winston had been on the trail for nearly a week. Far from the crowded cities, he was surrounded by the wilds. He was invigorated and relaxed in the sharp, earthy mountain air, intense sunshine, enveloped on all sides by a myriad of tall, green trees and steep, wet ground. He was alone in the habitat of the deer, elk, squirrels, cougar and bear. It was his habitat too, he felt comfort in the visceral sensuousness of the wilderness than anywhere else, like home.

Just as he had retreated to the safety of his family after his fasting and suicide attempt, he was now fleeing to an even greater protective environment. It was more than a home to Winston, it was holy ground. This is the place he would gather strength and mend his mind, a place anyone and everyone could recover from the wounds of a crushing culture that exits in the cities.

He was at a baseline. He would grow from here and emerge much stronger.

His journal entries continued daily.

June 26th: Writes of his philosophy and a long passage of his struggle with "what is left of the devil."

June 27th: Describes a beautiful hike over Ten Mile ridge and sets up camp at an elevation of 12,500 feet. Has "an amazing day" taking many photos of wildflowers. Discusses how "gifts from God" are far better than "stealing wealth." Writes a version of what happened to Mallory and Irvine, Englishmen who made an early attempt on Mount Everest and famously disappeared high on the mountain. Winston believes that Irvine "saw evil... that made him sick or completely insane." Mentions that he "wants to be with God and if dying is what it takes, I am willing... not by my hand but by God's hand."

This is the day, about one week into his trek that Winston's writing becomes less about daily trek life and more about his philosophy, good and evil and God and demons. Up to this time he mainly writes of the day-to-day happenings in the life of a wilderness trekker: The rain, the pesky mosquitos, the melting snow patches along the trail, the thick pine forests and blue lakes, Townshend's reaction to what she encounters and her difficulties, blisters and doggie pack strap failures. Up to this day he wrote more about the mysterious beauty of campfires, and of the ecstatic joy of eating a full meal.

But from this day onward, he becomes more and more focused on the abstract. The vast, wild, primordial wilderness overwhelms him with joy and he writes tirades against those who would destroy it for greed. He writes of the spiritual emptiness of that greed and consumerism and longs for our culture to become one with nature rather than one with the almighty dollar. And he writes of the battle in his mind between a more abstract good and evil. People are not the only entities he sees around him, there are also spirits.

June 28: Winston is hiking around the ski runs near the Breckenridge ski resort. He laments the destruction of the forest and notes the lodge below him. It is a powerful vision, the resort lodge is symbolically made of the forest that was destroyed to make a ski run. They are "spending what they did not earn." Makes camp beyond ski area and writes poetically about his campfire. He notes that camping is "therapy for the body and soul." Again hears drumming and now believes these are war drums.

June 29: Ecstatic about mountain scenery and further laments those who would destroy it for greed of money.

June 30: Near Tennessee trailhead. Begins a long tale of the Ute Indian "Three Bears" and the European "Redbeard." They contest each other then cooperate in gold smuggling. "All gold must be returned to the Earth."

Winston's tale of Three Bears and Redbeard begins and continues over several days of journal entries and is referred to throughout the rest of his journal. The tale goes roughly like this: The great Ute Indian warrior Three Bears encounters a skilled European mountain man Redbeard in an era sometime between when the Spanish arrived and colonized South America but before there is widespread European influence within the interior of North America.

Three Bears challenges Redbeard to a duel. Redbeard has a rifle; Three Bears a bow and quiver of arrows. They are tipped with arrowheads made of special stone. They stand several paces apart and shoot at each other simultaneously. Every single shot collides between them, arrow hitting bullet, attesting to the great but equal skill of each man.

Because they cannot defeat each other they conclude they must be made of the same great spirit. They decide to form an unusual alliance to smuggle gold, but this isn't your normal smuggling operation. It is in reverse. It is not for profit. They are to gather all the gold and smuggle it back to its origin in South American mines, return it to the earth from whence it came.

Three Bears and Redbeard go their separate ways to accomplish their shared mission. Years later, Redbeard encounters another great Ute named Two Crows, struggles with him and eventually kills him. When Three Bears next encounters Redbeard, he asks about his friend Two Crows. Redbeard admits to killing Two Crows so that "he could be one with him."

Redbeard had realized Two Crows was not a man but a magical being, and now Redbeard himself was a magical being. Three Bears reveals that he too is not a man but a spirit who speaks for God. Because of the great work Redbeard has done returning gold to it's origin, Three Bears grants Redbeard/Two Crows all the land around Mount of the Holy Cross, making it the spiritual ground it is today.

Winston's tale is much more rambling, but he consistently uses three metaphors: The bear is always a symbol for goodness or God himself. Gold is the symbol for greed and the rape of the earth or environment and must be returned to set the world right. Lastly, there is always a struggle not simply for good, but for the power to do good. You can't simply want to do good, you have to fight for the right to challenge and defeat evil.

June 30: Camping in Holy Cross wilderness. Hears what he thinks are horses go by his tent though he is far from trail. "Something keeps telling me to look for the crucifix."

Perhaps Winston is simply waxing spiritual, influenced by the name of the nearby mountain. Or perhaps something else is going on. His reference to horses and searching for a crucifix are steeped in the legends of what was once Colorado's most famous mountain, Mount of the Holy Cross. It is highly unlikely that Winston knew of the deep history of this area.

Holy Cross was named for the giant 1500-foot high geological feature that forms a rough crucifix shape on its eastern face. The feature is a near vertical gully running from the summit to the Bowl of Tears valley below. A nearly horizontal ledge system intersects the vertical gully in such a way as to form a large cross shape. The gully and ledges hold significantly more snow than the surrounding slopes and thus during summer snowmelt, the cross stands out in white relief on the otherwise darker rock on the mountain face.

The cross is not perfect in that the right arm is incomplete. And except for a few strategic locations, it is well hidden from view. The mountain itself is one of the more remote in Colorado. No roads pass close enough to see the mountain. A high ridge blocks the view of the cross from easily accessible nearby high points. Thus the best way to view the cross is to hike several hours to the summit of Notch Mountain, the singular location to enjoy a spectacular view of the cross.

Though the native Ute knew of the mountain and the cross feature, to the early Europeans Holy Cross only existed in legends. Early explorers were aware of the story of a mountain emblazoned with a large crucifix seen by Spanish priests in the 1700s. The legend told of how these priests, lost in a blizzard and close to death, kneeled down to pray for direction. The clouds parted to reveal the magnificent cross and pointed the way home.

Only when William Henry Jackson made his famous Holy Cross photos in 1873 was proof of this mountain seen by Europeans. The mountain soon evolved into a pilgrimage site and remained a destination for thousands seeking God for many decades. This ended when the U.S. military closed the area to the public just prior to World War II due to its proximity to Camp Hale, the high altitude training camp for the famous 10th Mountain Division.

Today, Mount of the Holy Cross is well known but retains a mysterious side unique to Colorado. Hikers loose their way on this mountain with alarming regularity. And like a high altitude Bermuda Triangle, some have vanished completely, never to be found despite intensive search efforts.

This area was not something Winston ever wrote or spoke about until he arrived on his trek. The probability that he knew of this history of this area is vanishingly small, yet somehow he sensed the ancient quest in search of the cross as well as the feeling that it was holy ground.

July 1: "Last night I went into a trance I didn't intentionally try to go into... I am under direct orders from God to find a silver cross, and I think I just might!" Describes hearing thunder, or a bear.

July 2: Climbs Mount Massive. Does not tread on "sacred ground" of the summit. Rambles about evil while there. "I can transmit and receive messages clearly, about as clearly as possible." Exaggerated significance of numbers reappears. Reluctantly writes about a "weird and personal" experience of being visited by Hosni Mubarak, who asks Winston to save the world (note: Three years before the Arab Spring). Writes of revelations from God of catastrophe, laments technology and the destruction of the Garden.

July 4: Climbs Mount Elbert, the highest mountain in Colorado. He drinks water out of "highest mountain lake, unfiltered, unzapped and un-sanitized and savoring every drop." Strange ramblings. "Roman Rothchild called me again last night and was trying to convince me he was the voice of God." Hallucinates about search and rescue team walking by his tent.

July 5: Admits he is "fine" on the trail but gets "mentally fucked up" when he comes back to "reality." Writes more of God and devils.

July 8: Strange ramblings about "the key." "You still remember that blazing image it made even after your eyes were taken away. That burning circle, no, how could you ever forget it for you too will burn on into antiquity."

July 10: Camping in Missouri basin. "Taking time to battle your demons."

July 11: "I am the one who destroyed evil and I did it without taking a life."

July 12: Near Buena Vista. Writes of God: "What do you want me to do, when the trail is over, when do I meet you?" Daily entries are becoming very lengthy.

July 13: Writes of battling demons, long rants insulting demons. Compares them to ticks. "This isn't a camping trip, it's a shootout with the devil. I didn't come here to build campfires and look at the stars, I came out there to track something down, to kill them, one by one, forty days, forty demons, some of them far easier than others, but today was especially hard."

July 14: "The devil has been beaten." Hitchhikes into Buena Vista and has dinner at a pizzaria. Long passages about God, Devil and the environment. Charges his camera battery but accidentally leaves charger plugged in at the restaurant.

Winston pens a letter to his sister in his journal on this day. He apologizes for "running away from her world... I'm trying to believe in God enough to stop this whole world from bleeding and if that's too much it still feels like not enough, but I have to keep on trying because that's what God says I'm supposed to do." He writes of how he loves all her family, including what he sees as their faults of living in the culture of consumerism.

He then writes of his confusion as to where to go next, as if he is at a three-way intersection with no direction sign. He's been hanging around Buena Vista for several days and feels the need to continue on the Colorado Trail. But he accidentally left his camera battery and charger in the pizza restaurant in Buena Vista. He would have to burn an entire day to again hitchhike back to town to pick it up, assuming it is still there, and feels he might have enough battery power to last until Durango anyway. And he feels a strange urge to return to the small lake where he had a strange experience.

It was at Kroenke Lake, northwest of the summit of Mount Yale and just below the Continental Divide. He writes that he,

> "...had already gone up there once, traveling light. But while I was up there someone was showing me around, especially that lake and surrounding vicinity, as if it would be a good place to stay if I ever came back. They showed me a camp spot with a metal grill, close to the trail and some snow and the lake, then had me climb above the lake to a perch full of quartz and had me sit up there."

It wouldn't be unusual for Winston to encounter someone at this lake. It is a well-known fishing hole that requires only a modest hike from the nearest trailhead. But his journal entry takes a twist as the person who showed him around disappears and apparently shape-shifts into a bear:

> "...Townshend had lost her front right shoe and I was looking for it with her and came across a steaming fresh pile of bear scat. I stuck my walking stick in and asked it to take me to the missing boot. It walked me out of the high scrub back onto the trail and down it about forty feet.

*And there it was sitting there, as if someone had
raced it there for me to find. It wasn't even close
to where I thought it would be."*

Once again Winston encounters a spirit-form bear that
guides him to a revelation, albeit a minor one. But this
encounter made an impression on Winston.

If he returned to Kroenke Lake, he would be delayed by a
few days and he wrote of confusion as to why he would even
want to return. He wrote, "who would want me up there and
why?"

July 15: Makes the decision to hike up to Kroenke Lake
after "an intense interaction with my childhood friend Jeff
Barian, helping him with his chakras, yoga and Kundalini." Has
conversations with people around the lake, he is not sure if they
are real or not. Writes of the sublime beauty of the small glacial
lake. Hears someone calling to him, saying "Parabola! I'm ready
to talk."

July 16: In a great mood. "13,000 feet, that's my hood,
we'll walk on it, touch it, breath it, smell it, wade in it, walk it
over then walk it again..." Mentions hot springs around Mount
Princeton and imagines a cataclysm that destroys everything
east of him. Writes about rings, loops, circles, three of
everything. Derisive comments about consumerism, "polish
your image but never touch your true spirituality." "Like I told
my friend Parabola, life isn't based on a parabolic curve, it is
more like the curve of the petal of a flower or a Mobius loop."

July 18: Hartenstein Lake. "God put me on this trip."
Writes of how he craves company for the first time since he
began his trek. Writes of admiration of women for the first time
in this journal. Confused as to what his purpose is. "Not what I
imagined it would be like." Prays to God to fix his creation.

A portion of Winston's Colorado Trail journal July 14th multi-page entry that illustrates his style of packed, margin-to-margin outpouring of ideas and experiences.

Winston wrote more than sixty thousand words in twenty-six days. He then packaged it up and mailed to Jovanka for safekeeping, and started a new journal.

Nothing is known about his experiences over the next one hundred and fifty miles of trekking. This is one of the most isolated sections of the Colorado Trail, far from even small towns in a sparsely populated expanse of the state. He spent a little over two weeks in this wilderness before arriving at the town of Creede, where he spent a few days resupplying and resting from the trail. He called Jovanka from Creede on August 5 and had a few items of mail delivered to him.

His next confirmed location was late August in Lake City, located about fifty miles northwest of Creede. Neither Creede nor Lake City lies on the Colorado Trail. Winston had gone off-route and would never return.

At The Threshold

Demons exist in their little cracks in time...

W.B.C.

August 28, 2008. Southwestern Colorado. Winston picked up the pay phone outside the Lake City Visitor's Center and dialed Jonathan Wrobel's number. It went to his voicemail. He left an ominous message, "Dude, I don't need anything anymore, thanks for everything." He then called Shanna and left a similar message and told her he was leaving Townshend tied up at the Visitor's Center, and could she make sure Townshend got to a good home?

As a manager of a Chicago area REI, Inc. store, Jonathan was able to help Winston get a tent, a jacket and other essentials for wilderness living. He continued to help re-supply him with packages containing essentials, such as backpacking food, replacement gloves, etc., to be picked up at post offices in small towns along the Colorado Trail.

Jonathan moved from Colorado to Chicago in 2007 to pursue a better job opportunity at REI but still kept in touch. At the time, Winston tried to convince Jonathan to move to Silverton where they would have unlimited opportunity to continue their backcountry adventures together. Jonathan liked the idea but found the job prospects in the small mountain village lacking. Unlike Winston, he found the trade-off of giving up his career unacceptable.

Jonathan was unaware of Winston shutting down his Mobius cafe and moving back to Lakewood. He had sent Winston a Christmas card, but it was returned, stamped "Unable to Deliver." He thought that was weird, but then in a strange coincidence a week later, Jonathan's girlfriend found out that Mobius was closed.

"It was odd. She was making conversation with a stranger at work [in Chicago] and this person mentioned the Mobius Cafe in Silverton and that it had shut down. It was rumored that Winston had moved to Moab."

Jonathan then called Winston's mother Mirjana, and that's when he found out about the "incident" with Winston in his Lakewood condo and that he was currently staying at Jovanka's house. Jonathan finally got in touch with Winston who told him of the big events of the past few months: His Kundalini awakening, his fasting, his book, his suicide attempt, and his spiritual quest.

"It was strange, he was never into religion before. He thought it was total B.S. and he really hated B.S."

A few weeks later Winston called Jonathan and asked for help on his Colorado Trail journey. "Out of nowhere, while I was on a trip to Pittsburgh, I get a call. 'I need your help Jonny, I want to hike the Colorado Trail,'" Jonathan explained.

"I thought, wow, this is crazy!"

"I bought a bunch of stuff for him to pick up at the REI in Colorado Springs. That's when I met Shanna. We both agreed to help Winston on his trek." Though Shanna had her doubts about the outcome of his trek, Jonathan thought it was a positive step.

"Winston loved the woods. They rejuvenated him. Also, I truly believe that being in nature is a kind of renewal for people."

But then two months later Winston left his last message on Jonathan's phone. After calling him he phoned Shanna. She listened to her voicemail later and became alarmed. She phoned the Lake City Visitor's Center and spoke with Steve Robertson. She described her concern that Winston may be in a bad emotional state and in trouble. Robertson had not seen Winston but was concerned enough to phone the sheriff Ron Bruce. Sheriff Bruce called Shanna, Jonathan and Jovanka and got the same message, everyone felt Winston was in trouble.

He had been hanging out in the Lake City area for several days prior to that. He was camping in the surrounding mountains but would walk into town just as he had done near Buena Vista. During a previous phone conversation with Jonathan, Winston said he was camping near Crystal Lake, located in a high valley a few miles due west of the tiny mountain town.

Realizing that he was just days from the Colorado Trail finish line in Durango, Jonathan asked, "What are your plans when you've finished?"

"I don't know," Winston replied.

"What about winter? Are you planning to hang out in Silverton with friends?"

"I'm not thinking about more than a day ahead," Winston admitted.

Lake City is the last town on the Colorado Trail before Silverton, a town filled with reminders of both cherished and terrible memories for Winston. Jonathan thinks this may have caused Winston to hesitate on his trek. Technically, the Colorado Trail passes south of Silverton and could be avoided altogether. But Winston stopped just short of it and hunkered down at Crystal Lake to consider his future. Or perhaps wait for further direction from God.

He picked up a package of supplies sent by Jonathan, but Winston was running out of cash. He called his sister and asked her to send his debit card for an account he had set up with his tax refund before he hit the trail. Jovanka had no idea that Winston had done this and had already stopped Winston's mail to his old address in Lakewood where the card would have been sent. She didn't have it and Winston didn't have any other way to get cash in Lake City.

The "disappearance" of money may have been interpreted by Winston in the same way the "appearance" of money had been two months prior; a sign from God. It meant something. Winston made his final calls to Shanna and Jonathan a couple days later.

He could have headed in any direction from Lake City. Jonathan told the sheriff he thought Winston might be in the area of Crystal Lake, his last camp, or possibly Uncompahgre Peak, but no one really knew. Sheriff Bruce and a deputy patrolled several roads and checked out trailheads as the sun was setting that evening. They came up empty.

The next morning Bruce filed a missing person's report and dispatched his volunteer search and rescue team, a dedicated group of fewer than ten volunteers. For two days they scoped the mountains and put up "missing person" posters with Winston's photo at trailheads, but as time went on the chances of finding him faded.

"It's a big country out there and nearly impossible to find someone in it who doesn't want to be found," Bruce admitted, so he called off the search. Though two days might seem like a fairly short time, Bruce really didn't have much more to go on and did not want to burn out his volunteers, who might be needed for another operation at any time, on what was likely a dead end.

That's when Jovanka, Shanna and Jonathan began pleading for help from backcountry enthusiasts via the Internet. Their postings reached thousands of people, many of whom might be hiking in the area. They set up a blog site to track of what had been searched and the clues that were found.

The blog site was titled "In Search of Winston." It grew rapidly as volunteers who had never heard of him reported where they had searched or put up posters that displayed a photo of Winston and read:

> We are sending out missing persons posters for our friend Winston whom we have not heard from for over three weeks. We have been in contact with Sheriff Ron Bruce of the Hinsdale County Sheriff's department, however, I want to make sure we cover as broad an area as possible so we are reaching out to the surrounding counties.
>
> Winston lived in Silverton, CO for many years until closing his coffee shop and moving back to Denver. He had been hiking the Colorado Trail for the past several months, he started in Denver, and his plan was to hike the full trail ending in Durango. He had been in fairly constant contact with both Shanna and Jonathan until the end of August when he left his dog in Lake City. He made two phone calls to Shanna and Jonathan letting them know he would not be needing any more food packages sent along the

```
trail and no one has heard from
him since.
```

The posters went up all around the town of Lake City, the Black Canyon near Gunnison, as well as Silverton and Ouray. People searched as far away as Grand Junction which lies about 100 miles north of Winston's last seen point and Monarch Pass, 100 miles east.

The first intriguing clue was a report from a searcher that had spoken with a sheepherder, a migrant worker who spoke little English. What this witness saw was included with the internet postings asking for help:

```
    ...When he was last seen, by
a sheep herder outside of Lake
City, he was reportedly no longer
continuing on the trail and was
hiking towards the West Elk
Drainage. He told the shepherd,
that he was planning on returning
to Lake City around the 8th of
September; he has not returned
since. He may [sic] continued on
to the Blue Creek Drainage
heading towards Cimarron and
continuing to Gunnison, but we
really have no idea. Ultimately,
we are unsure as where he was
heading.
```

This sighting was considered very credible and in retrospect did roughly indicate the direction from Lake City to where Winston was ultimately found. It also contains another interesting clue; it did not appear that Winston was headed into the wild to kill himself. Quite the contrary, he indicated that he would be returning to Lake City, perhaps to resupply.

An eerie post was made to the blog on October 12th:

> I manage land that was once part of the Tierra Amarilla Land Grant and is now commonly known as Banded Peak Ranches. I am also a licensed outfitter and lease most of the land each fall for Elk hunting.
>
> On Sunday October 12, 2008, a hiker walked into my camp following a road which comes into the main valley from the East fork of the Navajo River, west of the continental divide. It was a cold windy day with rain/snow showers.
>
> I walked up to him and began asking questions, wanting to know where he had come from and where he was going. I was not angry; I figured this guy was very lost and possibly in trouble. He did not want to talk to me, and did not stop walking. I walked beside him.
>
> He said he had come from Platoro, had been on the divide with friends who had horses, and had left them because of the snow. I asked him if he knew where he was. He said he had a map. I asked him to get it out

and I would show him where he was. He said it was buried in his pack. He said he was following the Navajo River. I told him that the river flows south and pointed out the road to take to follow the river to Chromo and highway 84. (He was headed north when I first saw him).

He was wearing black tennis/skateboarder type shoes, black nylon knee shorts with white stripes on the sides, a gray/black hooded sweatshirt jacket, with the hood up. His clothes looked worn and oily. He had a small daypack on with a black rolled-up sleeping bag tied to it. I saw a frying pan or cooking kettle handle sticking out of the bag. He had a plastic quart milk bottle with red lid (empty) tied on top of the bag. He and his gear were wet.

I offered him a bowl of hot soup beside a hot fire. He said he had food. (I think he was tempted). I offered to give him a ride to Chromo--it would be no trouble. He refused. I told him to stay on that road, take no turns, and he would come to Chromo. He walked on down the road.

> I would say he was somewhat incoherent; he was wet and cold and did not give me what I would call sensible answers.
>
> After he left I called a friend with the Archuleta Sheriffs department to ask him what more I could do. He sent a deputy and I think an ambulance out. I don't know what happened, but they did not see him. He followed the road a while, we saw his tracks, but he left it and vanished.
>
> The sheriff brought a photo of Winston and all of us in camp who saw him are positive that this was Winston.

The location described by this witness is just southwest of Alamosa where Winston's mother Mirjana lives, an area he knew well and hiked extensively. There was no follow-up to this sighting and despite the proximity to an area he was known to explore and matching physical description.

I asked Jonathan if Winston said anything about suicide or killing himself in his last message. "That's what Shanna and I both feared from the message but he didn't say he was going to kill himself. In fact do not think Winston was ever intending to kill himself," he said.

However, it did appear that Winston was going to attempt another dangerous excursion into the fog of transcendence, just as he did in Lakewood, but completely alone and isolated. This time he was in the wilderness and there would be no way to come back if he got too close to the edge, no way to dial 9-1-1 as he did in Lakewood.

Despite the efforts of so many people alerted by the web postings, there were no credible clues as to where he went. He was gone.

Last Days

...When we reached a point where
the ATVs could go no further,
they were secured and those folks
continued on foot. We then
reached a point that it was no
longer passable even for the
horses and they too were secured.
We noted a very large number of
downed trees from the micro-
bursts [violent thunderstorms]
experienced during the fall of
2008, blocking the trail.

Excerpt from *Recovery of Churchill's Body,*
Supplemental Report
Sheriff Ronald Bruce
July 16, 2009

Autumn 2008. Porphyry Basin, Colorado. The sheriff report of the recovery of Winston's body tells of the destruction caused by one or more major thunderstorms that swept Porphyry Basin while Winston camped there. The storm was violent enough to uproot numerous 100-foot tall healthy pine trees that had stood for hundreds of years.

Storms of this magnitude are rare and probably made a deep impression on Winston. Perhaps they were a foreboding sign to him, warning of the catastrophe to come. The sheriff only noted that the new treefall was making it difficult for him and his team to do their job.

Winston's decaying body was lying outside the cabin in Porphyry basin with his trekking poles placed neatly at his head. He was wearing winter clothing and lightweight boots. He was identified by his clothing and a season ski pass with his name and photo still attached to his jacket.

His hands appeared to have been severely frostbitten. One of his trekking poles had a sharp, forty-five degree bend at the tip. With him was a hip pack containing a pocketknife, a container of vitamin pills, a camera and what appeared to be his final journal.

He had been entombed beneath many feet of snow over the winter. The spring thaw then soaked everything. His final journal, stuffed in his water permeable pack and written in felt marker, was rendered unreadable. His camera was waterlogged.

His body was evacuated to the medical examiner's facility in Montrose. The coroner reports that an autopsy was performed that concluded he died of "hypothermia and starvation." No evidence of foul play was discovered, and the authorities had what they considered a positive identification, so the sheriff pursued no further investigation. The family agreed that no dental records or DNA identification was necessary and his body was cremated.

For the official investigators, the case was closed. An unprepared madman disappears in the mountains, dies at some point during the winter and his body is found the next summer by hikers. No foul play discovered. It doesn't happen every day but is common enough to be plausible.

But that wasn't the end of the story. Further evidence was found of what Winston experienced in Porphyry, why he was there and the likely reason for his death.

Winston's belongings were given to Jovanka. His final writings surely contained the reasons for his actions, but unfortunately they were destroyed. There were no clues to be found in the soaked pages. But also in his pack was his camera.

"The camera was completely full of water," Dennis lamented. Still, he thought it might be worth trying to recover whatever images it contained. He opened it to the air and dried it over several days. To his surprise, when he turned it on it still worked, and it contained 1,365 digital photos of the last months of Winston's life.

His photo record displays his fascinating and terrible journey. Most shots are what you would expect of a fun adventure along the Colorado Trail. There are hundreds of portraits of barren high peaks, snowfields, green forests and rivers, camp sites, sunsets, elk, foxes, flowers, insects and rocks.

He was bewitched by dead trees and the haunting shapes they made, like the skeletal remains of ancient tendriled and malevolent beings. He also took many photos of his campfire at night, orange flames leaping randomly from bright coals.

Like a photo-taking Van Gogh, Winston had a proclivity to make self-portraits. This was despite the fact that he rarely liked hardcopy photos of himself and in fact had burned most of them in the past. Rarely smiling, he appears pensive, serious and contemplative.

He took self-portraits relaxing along a creek bed with a beer in hand, a joint at the ready. Another photo shows him smoking a cigar, his long hair and beard reminiscent of Che Guevara. Another is above treeline as if on a summit, standing in front of a propped up log, his arms outstretched and head dropping to one side, evoking the image of Christ being crucified.

There is a date associated with each image. Winston made occasional photos of trail signs, showing where he was on certain dates. From this data, Dennis was able to piece together a map showing the progress of Winston on the trail between Denver and Lake City.

The photo journal shows that Winston approached Porphyry Basin from the south, trekking approximately twenty miles northwest of Lake City. He traversed over the 12,400-foot pass below the cliffed-out west face of Uncompahgre Peak and descended into Middle Cimarron Creek valley. Several miles down the valley, he turned right and ascended five hundred feet up into Porphyry Basin, a hanging valley draining into Middle Cimarron.

He made many photos in Porphyry, several of which show his tent and camp. The sheriff and investigators did not know about his tent, they had only searched for evidence around the A-frame. When Jonathan saw the digital photos, he thought they might be able to find the tent, if it was still there, based on its relationship to the mountains in the background.

"I found his tent when I visited the valley later that month [after Winston was found]," Jonathan described, "based on the photos in Winston's camera." It was mostly collapsed from the crushing winter snow, but one end was still standing. His sleeping bag was inside, soaked from the water. His small gas stove was upright with a cooking pot still resting on the burner. Except for the snow and water damage, the tent had been left as if the owner would soon return.

Winston's photo journal shows that he ascended to treeline in upper Porphyry Basin and camped near the creek running along the south side of high-altitude plateau. Located about a quarter mile above the cabin, this was the logical campsite in the basin, the trees offering a bit of wind protection and a water supply within a short walk from camp. But he didn't stay there.

One of the last photos found on Winston's camera. He made this self-portrait in his tent looking out at Porphyry Basin in late summer, just prior to his final fast.

The photo record shows that for some unknown reason, he moved to another campsite on the north side of the basin. This was an odd move. His campsite was no longer level and he was sleeping on an uncomfortably steep incline. His access to water was far more difficult. The closest creek on the north side of the basin was now three hundred feet below him, down a steep, awkward slope covered in loose rock. This last site is where Jonathan found the remains of Winston's camp.

Winston's last photos are a series of self-portraits documenting his progressing emaciation. On September 7th he begins to look haggard. Two weeks later his cheeks are sunken, his eyes bulging, skin wrinkled and his shoulder length hair has become a ropy tangle. He took two photos of himself in this state that are extremely disturbing. They are the images of a suffering, wasted madman beyond help, alone in the wild.

He was suffering physically and mentally, but based on his recent state and his experience of prior fasting, it is likely he was going through a vast spiritual transformation as well. His visions and demon-battles were probably growing in intensity as he approached his final near-death experience. He was riding his Kundalini energy to the next plane of existence.

But it was necessary to finish out this life first. He woke up every day knowing he would experience the physical suffering of his body but also ready for any spiritual revelations that he would receive. It was very slow and difficult. Of the suffering, "I think he chose starvation because it was pure," Jonathan told me, "and it shows the extreme mental fortitude that Winston had." Jumping off a cliff or even lying naked in a cold stream would have killed him much faster. But it wouldn't have been pure, and the purity would take away from his spiritual experience. He needed the forty days.

In his last photo, dated October 12, the day before his forty-first birthday, Winston is laying in his tent bundled in his sleeping bag. He is wearing his jacket and hat. There is a dusting of snow visible through the translucent fabric of his nylon tent. Only his face is visible, but he appears to be an old man. His face is skeletal, it appears there is nothing between his skin and skull. His eyes are huge and perfectly sane.

After his last photo, he used the video function of his camera to describe his final intentions. Inside his tent he could barely force the words out of his thin body. His last communication was:

It's October 12th
Day before my birthday
I was hoping I would die naturally
But it's not happening
So I'm going to kill myself tonight

I haven't eaten since the 2nd
That's close enough to 40 days.
It was a crazy trip.
I love you all
Bye bye

Despite what he says are his intentions, he did not die that night and probably lingered for many days, perhaps weeks longer. There is significant evidence to support this conclusion. The first clue is from Sheriff Bruce when he reported that Winston's hands "appeared to be severely frostbitten."

Frostbite is what happens when ice crystals form in the tissue causing damage. The tissue has to actually freeze to produce frostbite, not just get cold. If you walk outside on a "freezing" winter night of thirty-five degrees Fahrenheit, you cannot develop frostbite. You may develop hypothermia, a dangerous lowering of body temperature, but frostbite is impossible if the temperature remains above the freezing point of water.

Even if the temperature is below thirty-two Fahrenheit degrees, the freezing temperature of water, you are still unlikely to suffer from frostbite unless you are exposed for a relatively long period of time. The body has a natural heating system that keeps your tissue warm for a while, but not forever. Heat is delivered to all of your tissue via your blood.

If your body is not generating enough heat through normal metabolism or exercise, it will soon shut down circulation to "non-essential" body parts that are losing heat in an attempt to preserve your core temperature as long as possible. Your extremities lose out to your internal organs. Fingers, toes, ears and nose are first to go. Then hands, feet, legs, arms, genitals. As circulation shuts down, there is nothing left to warm the tissue and freezing sets in.

It is possible for frostbite to form within minutes, but only with unprotected flesh in severely cold environments. In

Antarctica, where it may be forty degrees below zero with a sixty mile-per-hour wind, you want all exposed flesh to be covered or it will freeze within seconds. But in the relative mildness of the Colorado Mountains in autumn, it is unlikely that severe frostbite can develop in less than a day.

When frostbitten tissue is still frozen, it appears white or grayish due to lack of circulation. When re-warmed, purple or black blisters form and dark bruising becomes apparent. It is important to note that blood circulation is necessary to develop the blackened and blistered appearance of frostbitten tissue. A dead body has no circulation and so cannot form this appearance. Therefore, Winston must have been alive when he developed the frostbite in his hands.

Because Winston was fasting he was far more susceptible to frostbite due to his lowered metabolism and inability to generate heat, and frostbite may have progressed more rapidly in him. But still it was not likely that Winston had frostbite when he made his last photos and video. Though his hands are not visible, there is no sign of frostbite on his nose, something very likely if he were slowly succumbing to the elements.

Also, severe frostbite would render Winston's hands nearly useless. He would have lost his manual dexterity due to both numbness and severe pain. Because of the tissue damage, his skin would lose integrity and scrape off or stick to whatever he touched or tried to manipulate. Working the zippers on his tent, sleeping bag and jacket would become an excruciating and gory task. He would not be able to write or manipulate the tiny controls on his camera.

Because his body was shutting down and the nights were getting colder, Winston might have developed frostbite over several days or possibly even weeks after he made his final video. There was further evidence that Winston was dealing with frostbitten hands in his last days.

Jonathan found it while examining the remains of Winston's camp. "There was bloody gauze on the floor [of the tent]." I asked what else he found. "Well, it was strange. His cooking pot had something crystalized on the edges. I'm pretty sure it was urine. I speculate that in the end, he didn't have the strength to hike the hundred feet or so down to the creek and might have become so uncomfortable with his thirst that he drank his urine." It was a disturbing addition to the already horrific suffering of starvation he endured.

"There was one other thing," Jonathan said after a moment of hesitation. "There were several opened condoms strewn on the floor. I have no idea what that meant."

I related to Jonathan my search and rescue group experience of finding the bodies of people who have died alone in the backcountry. When people get into a state near death they often take unexplainable actions. Victims of hypothermia are found nude, having stripped off their clothing just prior to death. Who knows why, except that an extremely cold person loses their rational thought processes as their body temperature drops. Perhaps something analogous happened to Winston in his final hours.

Or it could have been completely rational. He was trying to manage progressive frostbite of his hands using what he had available. Winston was found without gloves, he may not have had gloves for his summer trip, or he may have lost them along the way. He did have gauze in his first aid kit and apparently carried a supply of condoms.

Blood and other bodily fluids would have been oozing from his damaged flesh. It could be that having used up what little gauze he had available, he resorted to putting condoms over his oozing fingers. This would allow him to work a zipper, turn a stove knob or even handle his cooking pot without sticking to it.

Winston left his camp intact before he wandered a quarter mile down the slope to the A-frame. There, he lay his trekking poles on the ground and then lay down himself in front of the door, with his final journal in his small pack, and passed away.

His long-suffering journey was finally complete and he could rest.

The only question remaining was, why?

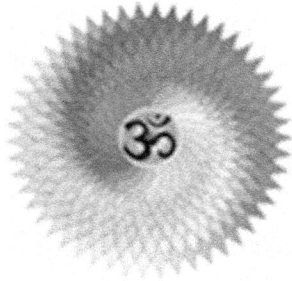

A Greater Cause

*... the Mayans and the Incas had told the Indians
that all gold must be returned to the earth, it was
of crucial importance to the saving of our planet.*

Excerpt from *Three Bears and Redbeard*
Colorado Trail Journal
W. B. C.

Winston's saga caught my interest when I saw the web posted pleas to be on the lookout for him. Given his background, I'd completely discounted that he could not take care of himself in the wilderness. He was obviously an expert outdoorsman. I had, however, seen my share of similar suicidal individuals during my decade long stint as a mountain search and rescue volunteer. Most of the time the sad story would end when we found a body and every time the method was relatively quick.

But after the discovery that he'd committed suicide by starvation, I knew there was far more to his story than most realized. That was radically different than anything I'd ever experienced or even heard about.

Of all the methods of suicide, killing oneself by starvation is exceedingly rare. Called apocarteresis, this is the method of suicide almost universally committed by those who see it as a sacrifice for a greater cause. An example is a hunger strike until death. It has also been practiced for religious reasons as a way to die in a "morally pure" state. Others have committed apocarteresis when faced with an inevitable death such as terminal cancer.

Winston had no terminal illness. He had recently begun a new spiritual venture. But of these reasons, dying for a cause seemed to fit Winston to a "T." He had a cause, a very big cause. He spoke and wrote of his cause relentlessly.

It is a horrific way to die. Starvation is an exceedingly slow process. As soon as a person stops eating, the body begins using its energy reserves of glycogen stored in the liver and muscles. These reserves are used up relatively quickly. A marathon runner, for example, will burn through his glycogen reserve in less than two hours. Even a sedentary person could burn through their reserve in less than a day. Hunger pangs generally begin long before this reserve is used up.

When stored glycogen is depleted the body then begins to break down fat and muscle tissue. This process can continue for many weeks as this tissue contains vast amounts of useable metabolic energy. Vitamin deficiency problems, such as scurvy caused by a lack of vitamin C, can occur during this stage of starvation if no vitamin supplements are taken. We know that Winston did take vitamins and probably did not suffer these maladies.

Though hunger is always present, atrophy of the stomach soon dulls the early pangs of starvation. However, other symptoms begin to appear such as weakness, fatigue, and muscle pain. Mental functioning deteriorates, rendering the victim apathetic and withdrawn. Finally, after a time that is usually longer than a month, the victim will lose consciousness and die when a vital organ such as the heart fails due to an utter lack of energy.

This was the second time in six months that Winston went on an extended fast. His long fast in his Lakewood condo was not begun as a suicide. That evolved near the end of his fast, perhaps as the result of the mental state induced by starvation, but it was not in fact the reason for his fast. It is worth noting that he understood very well the extended suffering he would endure again. And yet somehow he had the mental resolve to go through with it.

It did not seem possible to me that all of this could be spawned purely out of madness. Delving deeper into the mystery of the last days of Winston, I found what I thought was the undeniable motivation for his suicide; it was his last desperate attempt to broadcast his message to change the world.

The A-frame near where Winston was found is unusual in these parts. There isn't another livable mountain cabin within fifty miles. It's not that cabins or mine structures are unusual in Colorado, but most of the old mines and support buildings are decaying and dangerous remnants. Useable cabins, meaning that they have been built or maintained over the years, are all accessible by road, almost without exception. There is no road into Porphyry Basin and never has been. It is located in a designated wilderness area.

The spur trail up from Middle Cimarron ends at the cabin. There is no lake up there for fishermen, no hunting allowed, no compelling peaks to climb for mountaineers. The trail is shown on maps, but given the lack of destination attractions (except for the cabin), there is little reason to hike up this spur except for the pure enjoyment of nature.

Winston may have randomly wandered up to the only cabin in the wilderness area, but that seems very unlikely. Winston's journals showed that he was deliberate in his direction, always aimed for a mountain or a lake or a hot spring.

I believe Winston knew of the cabin before he left Lake City, and it was in fact his destination.

The A-frame was originally built in the 1890s but has undergone modern structural upgrades. Its foundation is now solid concrete though its roof is sagging. The interior is cramped, being a two hundred square foot single room with a small loft above. It is rustic, without electricity or plumbing. Water must be carried about fifty feet from the nearby creek. An outhouse stands nearby.

Of the more than thirteen hundred photos Winston made on his trip, including those of old broken-down structures he encountered on his journey, he did not take a single photo of this A-frame. It appears that he stayed in this hanging valley for up to six weeks and yet not a single photo of the A-frame. It was not even unintentionally shot as part of a background in the dozens of photos he took in the basin. Not one.

Yet I don't believe he was ignoring its existence. I believe quite the opposite, he knew of the A-frame as well as something else that was just downhill of the cabin. It was something that represented the cancerous greed of society and destruction of his wilderness holy ground. Something that was anathema to him, something that he would hate with every fiber of his being, the Robin Redbreast gold mine.

The Robin Redbreast mine has a surprisingly rare distinction. It is the only workable mining claim in the Uncompahgre wilderness area. And Winston, the anti-consumerist, enraged by any kind of wilderness destruction, just happened to end up in the same neighborhood.

The Robin Redbreast is not your stereotypical cavern big enough to drive a railcar through. Right now it is a horizontal 6-inch wide hole drilled into the side of a hill, barely noticeable except for the gasoline motor the size of a car engine that drives a drill shaft. It is far smaller than the remnant mines that pepper the San Juans, most having been abandoned more than a century ago.

But this is only the exploratory stage, the beginning of what could be a large operation involving blasting, continuous helicopter flights, surface water pollution and acres of tailings from a rent in the earth in an area most assumed would be protected from such violent destruction.

Wilderness areas are specially designated by the federal government. All forms of mechanized travel are forbidden. Bicycles are not allowed. In fact, any form of wheeled travel is banned. The rules are so strict that it is technically illegal to push a wheelbarrow along a trail in a wilderness area.

Nonetheless, the Robin Redbreast claim can be mined using, at least in theory, any mining technique deemed necessary, including the most destructive strip mining, restrictions on mechanisms be damned.

The Robin Redbreast is owned by Robert and Marjorie Miller, both in their 80s. Marjorie's father staked the claim in 1938, twenty-six years before congress passed the Wilderness Act, a law that attempts to preserve some of the last wild areas in the country from just this sort of destruction.

To gain critical support for the act, congress conceded to allow current active mining claims to continue. Through the decades the Miller's have kept their claim alive and now, due to modern industrial technology, a new and potentially large operation at Robin Redbreast is possible. Heavy blasting, continuous droning of machinery, tailings of towering rock piles, and the associated exhaust and water contaminated with heavy metals may be the fate of this pristine basin.

Winston would have surely abhorred the thought of a new working gold mine raping this wilderness. To him, this mine would represent the greedy chase of material wealth while simultaneously destroying the sacred ground of respite and atonement. It would be the same as tearing down an ancient temple to make way for a casino.

Massive destruction would be inflicted under normal operating conditions of a modern gold mine, but there is a greater danger. There is a real potential for a large-scale ecological disaster, one that may neither be neither preventable nor reversible if it happens.

There are precedents for this kind of disaster all over Colorado, but perhaps the most poignant happened in the early 1990s in the mountains just seventy-five miles southeast of Porphyry Basin. It was the Summitville Mine disaster.

Gold was first discovered at Summitville, a site located in the mountains a few miles southeast of Wolf Creek pass, in 1870. The discovery attracted several hundred prospectors who, using the best technology of the time, extracted more than eight tons of pure gold.

The Summitville Mine is located at an altitude of 12,500 feet and received thirty feet of snow over the winter. Avalanches and landslides were common. These harsh and dangerous conditions, along with a decreasing yield, resulted in the mine being abandoned by the early 1900s. It appeared the mine would forever remain a scar on the land, no better but no worse than the hundreds of abandoned mines that pepper the Colorado mountains.

However, in 1984 a Canadian venture invested several million dollars to use modern techniques in an attempt to extract gold from both newly strip-mined ore and existing tailings. The technique was to build large, vinyl-lined basins, fill the basins with ore and then spray cyanide over the ore to leach out the gold.

It was a successful operation. By 1990 the cyanide leaching technique extracted 294,365 ounces of gold and 319,814 ounces of silver worth well over $100 million at the time. Unfortunately, the vinyl in the leaching basins had torn, leaking acidic, heavy metal laden water into the streams draining from the site. This contamination spread down the Alamosa river, killing all aquatic life along a seventeen-mile stretch of a once pristine river.

When the corporation operating the mine was confronted by state officials about the leaking basins, they immediately declared bankruptcy and walked away, leaving a massively contaminated site. If it ever gets cleaned up, and it may not, the taxpayers will be footing the bill.

Case study material from American University in Washington D.C. summarizes the disaster that followed:

> The Summitville Mine in southwestern Colorado is a Superfund site of the federal Environmental Protection Agency. The EPA took over supervision of the mine at the request of Colorado mining regulators after the most recent operator of the 1,400-acre gold and silver mine, Galactic Resources Ltd. of Canada, walked away from the site and filed for bankruptcy late in 1992, leaving behind acid mine drainage and a 160-million-gallon containment filled with cyanide-laden water that threatened to spill over the earthen berm holding it back.
>
> It is estimated that the restoration of the site to an environmentally acceptable state will cost $120 million [this is greater than the value of all the extracted gold and silver - ed]. Attempts to garner some portion of those costs from Galactic Resources Ltd. thus far have been

unsuccessful, though the firm's former chairman, Robert Friedland, is involved in a number of other mining ventures around the world and is reported to be worth at least $400 million on paper as a result of one venture in eastern Canada. Friedland has contended that he cut his ties with Galactic prior to its bankruptcy and maintains that he has no knowledge of the environmental problems at the Summitville site. According to records obtained by The Denver Post, Friedland is a subject of a federal grand jury probe of the Summitville pollution. A grand jury in 1995 indicted two former mine managers; a guilty plea was entered to charges of 40 environmental crimes from Summitville Consolidated Mining Co., the mine's corporate owner.

The mine operators obviously did not intend to induce an environmental disaster, but the law of unintended consequences caught them. Because this was a modern, large-scale industrial operation, the strip mine itself covered an entire mountain, the disaster it produced was itself massive as well. And in the end the owners pocketed tens of millions in profit and walked away.

For Winston, there would be no moral complexity about the Robin Redbreast, it would be as simple as good versus evil. He would have hated this operation. And there is good evidence that Winston knew of the mine and the cabin before he arrived in Porphyry and that it was his objective.

The sheriff report that details his case, from the time of the first missing persons report to the final disposition of Winston's remains, contains an enigmatic passage: "Churchill is believed to have previously known of the cabin's existence." In that case it is highly likely he knew of the mine's existence.

The public record does not elaborate on this claim. However, as this was an official law enforcement investigative report, this statement is likely a summary of other evidence or witness reports that are not part of the public record.

Protests against the mine were heating up in the summer of 2007, when Winston was in full swing operating Mobius in Silverton. An article appeared in the magazine *High Country News* in May of 2007 describing the efforts of the mine owners to start up operations, and the protests that followed. Titled *A Gold Mine in the Colorado Wilderness?* by Morgan Helm, it began:

> A grandfathered mining claim passed down through generations has trumped the Wilderness Act. For the mine owners it's a victory; for others the potential mine raises concerns over wilderness protection and mining regulations.

The article goes on to describe that the owners expected to remove twenty five hundred tons of rock from the mountain to extract $6 million in gold, which is equivalent to $20 million in 2011 prices. This is quite a windfall for the owners who have been sitting on the claim for more than fifty years.

Protests were rallied by a local environmental organization called the High Country Citizens Alliance. The HCCA's mission is to "champion the protection, conservation, and preservation of the natural ecosystems within the Upper Gunnison River Basin." Their approach is through scientific studies to back legal methods of preservation through regulation. This highly active group had consistently protested the permitting process for the Robin Redbreast for many years and in 2007 was rallying local citizen support.

Both Lake City and Silverton were communities near the mine. From media articles and advertisements, to small town kiosks, to discussions among the locals, it would be hard to imagine that Winston was not aware of these developments. Even if he had simply overheard a conversation either in Mobius or later at the Lake City visitor's center, the subject would have triggered a strong reaction in Winston.

What would he have done in protest of this situation? There was no point in monkey wrenching because there was no mine yet. The cabin was there but vandalism had not been part of Winston's personality since he damaged the country club golfing greens as a young teenager in New Hampshire. Logic dictates only one reasonable course Winston would have taken. He would want to make a big splash, to get attention but in an honorable and pure manner.

And there was one other thing that brought immediacy to the situation, an indication that the mine opening was imminent. It was something that may have driven Winston to take drastic action. The A-frame was occupied by caretakers.

Sheriff Bruce stated in his report that there is no evidence that Winston had gone into the unlocked cabin. That is an unusual statement given that curious hikers are likely to peek inside just to take a look around. There is a note tacked just inside the door inviting visitors to look around but pleading with them not to steal the mining tools stored there as they are hard to replace. Why wouldn't Winston have stayed there, even if just for a few nights?

Robert Miller, owner of the cabin and mine, had the answer. I spoke with him about the events of the summer of 2008. After a long diatribe about the difficulties the Forest Service is placing on him in his attempt to ramp up his mining operation, he told me about the cabin.

"We have always kept it unlocked in case someone needs it for survival up there," Miller told me. "It is always stocked with food, a stove and fuel."

I asked him what he thought of the events surrounding the hiker whose body was found outside his cabin door.

"Oh yes, Harry spoke with him several times. He told him not to camp near the cabin." The sheriff's report did not mention anyone being in the basin at the time Winston was up there, and there was no evidence in Winston's photos. I asked Miller about this mystery man. "Harry and his wife lived up there that summer."

As part of his efforts to restart his operation, Miller hired Harry Castle, a retired miner in his 60s, to stay in the cabin and begin the preliminary work of assessing the mine. Harry and his wife rode horseback up to the cabin in August and moved in at about the time Winston was camping above Lake City. Harry had been living in the cabin for a month before Winston arrived in the basin.

Castle was forced to descend that autumn when he became seriously ill. He checked in to a hospital where his condition worsened and he entered into a coma. He was on his death bed. His wife, extremely upset that Winston was later found dead outside the cabin where they lived for weeks, refuses to discuss the situation. It is likely that Winston and Harry had more than one conversation about the mine.

It is possible that the Castles, from traditionally conservative blue-collar backgrounds, were not comfortable with a ragged, long-haired solo hiker with strange ideas about philosophy, society, money and God, camping somewhere above their cabin every night. They were a long way from help.

Miller explained, "Harry was an alcoholic but hadn't had any whiskey for years. I believe he started drinking again up there and that caused him to get sick." Because of his grave illness, Harry and Nancy left the cabin sometime in September. Whether Winston, a quarter mile above in his camp, was aware of the departure of the caretakers or not, he had chosen a course of action from which he would not deviate.

The official speculation was that Winston lay down to die near the A-frame so that he would be found in order for his family to have closure. This is a comforting boilerplate story that search and rescue officials tell a mourning family. Though possible, this is not a solid story in Winston's case.

Never in his life had Winston been concerned about telling his family or friends his situation or whereabouts. Jovanka complained that her brother would rarely send holiday cards or letters. He did not tell Shanna about Mobius until years later. He had little contact with Jonathan after he moved to Chicago. And not a soul knew he was living in his Lakewood condo, having his Kundalini awakening, fasting and eventually attempting suicide.

Also, Winston could have easily walked down the basin to the main trail in the Middle Cimarron valley, a trail that sees far more hiker traffic, and lay down there. If he had simply wanted his body to be found for closure, that would be a more likely scenario. But he did not do this either.

I believe he did want his body to be found, but for another reason.

Winston forced himself to die a natural death, a purifying death, intentionally lying near the defilement of his holy ground: The mine. It was symbolic of all wilderness destruction for greed. This was his protest, his great cause for which he was willing to die.

Winston did not begin his Colorado Trail journey to specifically end up dying in protest of a mine. He did, though, set out with an understanding that was born of his Kundalini awakening, and that he would be called upon to do something big. Something for his cause. Something to change the world. And he found it.

His writing, his philosophy, his death by starvation, and his location all point to this message.

The last year of Winston's life was a roller-coaster journey. Through the closing of his beloved Mobius cafe, the manic writing of his voluminous manuscript, his struggles with Kundalini awakening, desperately attempting to connect with God, fasting to near death, commitment to a psychiatric hospital, recovery, hiking the Colorado Trail to his final struggle with starvation and death in a likely protest to the rape of the wilderness, he fought a great battle within himself.

Regaining that primordial connection with nature was key. He wanted to go big time, to bring everyone to this understanding at once, and he grew frustrated at his lack of ability to accomplish this and turned his attention inward.

In his ever-consuming quest for spiritual insight, Winston appeared to become drawn to the near death experience, something that likely overwhelmed him. His early experimentation with the psychedelic substance DMT opened a door that changed his perception of life. Years later, his spontaneous Kundalini awakening exacerbated this perception and sent him toward his fate.

A Kundalini awakening can easily invoke the near death experience: The feeling one is about to die, the presence of an omnipotent being, moving through a tunnel toward a light, blissfulness and universal connectedness, and the border of no return.

As with DMT, the Kundalini awakening allowed Winston to venture to that psychological edge without real mortal danger to his body. Winston did not stop with the psychological experience of near-death, he pushed himself to actual brink of death on his forty day fast in Lakewood.

Each of these events changed Winston in a radical new way. The DMT experience left him fascinated, the Kundalini awakening left him maniacally seeking God, and the Lakewood fasting pushed him through the door of being willing to accept anything God wanted of him. Through it all, he maintained his belief of wilderness being the connection to the great spirit and consumerism being the great evil.

Coincidentally, during the last month of his life, gasoline prices were at an all-time high. Hoards of greed-driven financial jackals caused the housing market bubble to burst, the stock markets to crash, and humongous banks to fail. Unemployment was skyrocketing. Personal bankruptcies and foreclosures mounted. The net worth of the working class dropping by trillions of dollars. The deepest worldwide economic crisis in 70 years, the Great Recession, had begun with no end in sight. Much of it blamed on a runaway culture that has elevated the pursuit of money, status, and greed above all else.

Porphyry

... I'll keep on believing even after the funds run out, and the food, and they might, cause I ain't leaving without seeing what you're all about ... Please don't forget about me and all we've done, cause I don't want to die if no one's listening, and I don't want to leave all those crying voices behind, if you hear me then I have hope, but if I don't think you do then I am doing all this screaming for nothing, I don't need to know you or that you even exist, just fix it and do it some good, this is your creation, I just know you wouldn't just let it all slip by, because somehow we're all connected.

Colorado Trail Journal of W. B. C.
Somewhere near Mount Yale
July 18, 2008

October 13, 2009. Mirjana Churchill, Jovanka and Dennis Mersman, Robert Churchill, Shanna Rivera and her fiancé Charles "Chuck" Krausz, Jonathan Wrobel and his fiancé Inga Storbakken, Shawn Heinrichs, Padriaic "Paddy" Hannon and his fiancé Jennifer Kriske, gathered at the Cimarron Creek Middle Fork trailhead on what would have been Winston's 42nd birthday. It was overcast and chilly as they posed bundled in heavy coats for a group photo. Their goal was Winston's final camp, and with them they carried a heavy burden.

It was a long day for Jovanka, who was not used to hiking up steep mountain sides in the rarefied air of the San Juan Mountains. After several hours, the clouds gave way to the crystal blue sky of a perfect autumn day. There was no snow on the ground. Guided by Jonathan, they finally arrived, sat and rested for a long time. "That hike was really steep," Jovanka remembered, "but it's a very beautiful place."

Much like the days Winston spent there alone in his tent, the basin was wide open and silent except for the group of eleven loved ones. At his final campsite, they placed a specially prepared stone they had carried from the trailhead and said their goodbyes to Winston. His brother Robert knelt on one knee, placed his hand on the stone and nodded his head toward Precipice Peak for his moment of silence. Very few others would see the memorial, but it would stand as Winston did in his most cherished times of his life, alone in the wild.

Mirjana, Jovanka, Robert and Dennis soon began to gather and pack their gear for the long, but much easier, downhill hike back to the trailhead.

The rest were going to camp for a night in the basin as the friend they loved did, to connect with the wilderness in the environment of Winston's final days. They set up tents and raised a glass in honor of their compadre. Jonathan related the events that followed:

"It was a crazy night in the basin. There was definitely something surreal about the experience. As the sun was setting, it started to get windy and we knew a storm was coming. We joked that it was Winston trying to mess with us. After everyone went to sleep, Shawn and I stayed up stoking the fire, drinking cognac and sharing Winston stories. We laughed and cried till late into the night."

"The thunderstorm blew through and surrounded the basin. It was flashing so bright it was as if it was day for a split second and then completely black. It was a very crazy storm, tons of lightening and wind. The storm seemed to surround us, but never landed directly on us. It started to hail and rain, but only for a little bit of time. Shawn and I sat out through most of it and we both agreed, it surely was Winston trying to tell us that he was here with us."

The crescendo passed and the storm faded into the dark distance leaving a cold, calm night sprinkled with bright stars.

The next day they packed up and one by one they moved down the slope, leaving only a few footprints. The deep snows of winter would soon erase all signs of their passage. As their shuffling boots faded down the trail, Porphyry became silent once again.

The memorial was a natural, unremarkable rough stone that melded perfectly into the landscape, except for a soaring eagle and message engraved in the face:

"It was a crazy trip!"

Epilog

September 2010, Porphyry Basin. I paid a visit to Porphyry Basin two years after Winston. It was an eerie and revealing journey. The two hundred and fifty mile trip from my home in Boulder to the Middle Cimarron trailhead, the last thirty of which are on a rutted dirt road, didn't leave me enough time to hike up to the basin. I set up camp near the trailhead, a wild and lonely place. The last people I had seen were twenty miles back toward the main road.

Late that night I woke up and exited the tent. The stars twinkled brightly in the chill air and there wasn't a sound other than me walking over branches and leaves. At that moment I felt a presence and thought I could see a face through the trees, standing about one hundred feet away. The hair on the back of my neck rose. But as I looked more closely, I could see that it was an illusion caused by the tangle of willow branches and the faint shadows cast by the starlight. I walked over to the location and there was no sign that a human or animal had recently been there. The night was absolutely silent.

I returned to the tent. I've spent literally years of my life living in a tent in places all over the planet, and I am firmly grounded in the physical world, not believing in visitations by ghosts or spirits, so I quickly wrote it off to my subconscious imagination. But it was hard to forget.

The next morning was a crisp, beautiful autumn day. I hiked a little over an hour up the Middle Cimarron to the intersection of the Porphyry Basin trail. Ascending steeply out of the valley, the trail follows several switchbacks through a dense evergreen forest.

Thirty minutes up the trail is a two hundred foot waterfall. Just beyond the waterfall the basin opens up to a hanging valley of alpine tundra and peaks rising steeply, reaching up to the heavens.

The A-frame is still open to "those who need to use it as an emergency shelter," as Robert Miller stated. It is stocked with a bit of food, a gas stove and fuel. No one was living there and it's hard to imagine spending much time within its claustrophobic confines.

The Robin Redbreast Mine is not currently operational and expansion plans have been stalled mainly due to rules imposed by the Forest Service on the owners. The Forest Service is requiring that a new and much improved trail be constructed before mining operations begin. This has apparently given pause to the owners but in no way has taken the mining possibility off the table.

Summer 2011, Silverton: After Winston shut down Mobius in 2007, new owners opened up a coffee shop in the same site in Silverton, naming it the Steel and Steam Cafe and operated it for three years under that name. Ownership recently changed hands once again. The current owner has named it the Mobius Cafe.

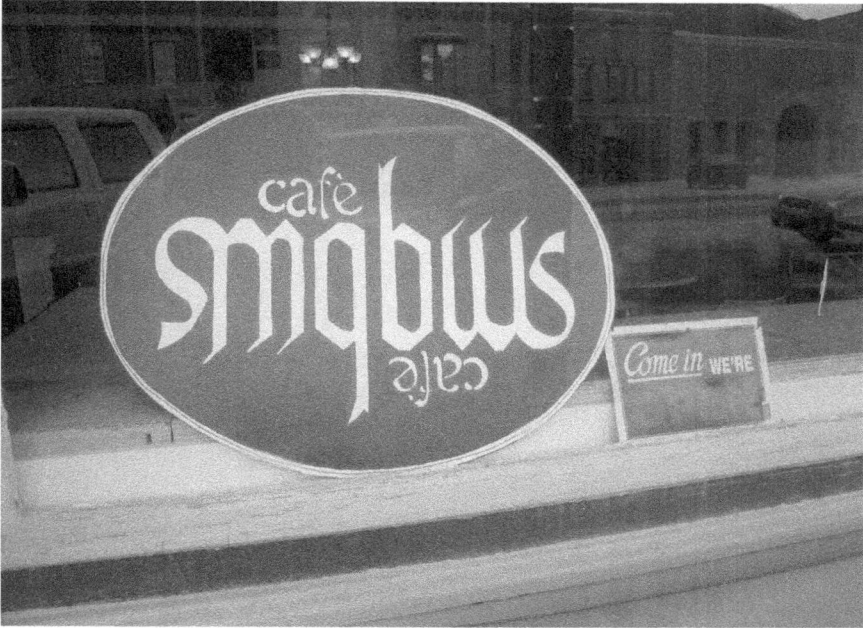

Sign in the window of the Mobius Cafe in Silverton, December 2011. (Scott Papich Photo)

References

The Psychology of Kundalini Yoga: Notes of the Seminar Given in 1932 by C. G. Jung, edited by Sonu Shamdasani, Princeton University Press, 1996.

Kundalini: The Evolutionary Energy in Man by Gopi Krishna, Shambala Publications, 1997.

DMT: The Spirit Molecule by Rick Strassman, M.D., Park Street Press, 2001.

Acknowledgements

I would like to thank Jovanka Mersman, Dennis Mersman, Jonathan Wrobel, and Shanna Rivera for their candid and sometimes painful recollections of Winston, especially those from the last year of his life.

I would like to thank Gillian Collins, Amanda Papich, Scott Papich, Caroline Stepanek, Joseph Stepanek, Shelly Scott-Nash, Jack Zuzack, and Marie Zuzack for their reviews and commentary about how to tell this story.

About the Author

Mark Scott-Nash has written about the human experience with the wilderness for many years and is the author of two previous books: *Colorado 14er Disasters: Victims of the Game* and *Playing for Real: Stories from Rocky Mountain Rescue.* He lives in Boulder, Colorado.